"An enforcer on the ice, he faced uns[...]
lost his will to reach for his ultimate [...]
impossible. Imagine people staring a[...]
skin. Imagine them calling you names. Now imagine enduring that for
15 years while playing a game you love. . . . Today, Val is finding his feet
again, without an ounce of bitterness. Instead, he tries to share his
experiences with the next generation, and sees a world where people are
not so quick to judge, to label, to hate. . . .What a remarkable journey."
— Harris Faulkner, *Fox and Friends* on the Fox News Channel

"[Val James] wrote a terrific book . . . this story is about overcoming
adversity . . . this story is a miracle. Read the book!"
— Stan Fischler, MSG Network

"This is a fantastic book, just amazing . . . there's a lot of good stories in
these pages. Check it out."
— Steve Mears, *NHL Live* on the NHL Network

"[James] recounts tales from his playing days with gusto."
— *The Buffalo News*

"*Black Ice* is an engaging read that sheds some important light on the
subject of racism in hockey. James is an entertaining narrator, and his
story is certainly one worth spending some time with."
— *Winnipeg Free Press*

"[Val James's] biography offers the same hard-hitting, bare knuckles
fighting approach he adopted in order to advance to the highest levels of
pro hockey. His story is one that is both highly improbable and hugely
entertaining . . . *Black Ice* is a fascinating story of an individual who
showed tenacity and courage in amassing a lengthy hockey career."
— *The Sherbrooke Record*

"James comes across as eloquent and thoughtful on his role and his
responses to racism."
— *Los Angeles Times*

"*Black Ice* does not read as a sad tale of 'should haves,' but as a proud story of accomplishment; a story of a man who played pro hockey and enjoyed almost every moment of it . . . James may have been the first African American to play in the NHL, but that's just a small part of his fascinating story."

— PuckJunk.com

"Bigotry sucker-punched him four decades ago before the start of a hockey tournament for 13-year-olds. As former Rochester Americans tough guy Val James recounts in his compelling new autobiography, *Black Ice*, his life would never be the same. Just as James didn't pull any punches while policing hockey games, he didn't hold back while writing *Black Ice*."

— Scott Pitoniak for *Rochester Business Journal*

"*Black Ice* tells about how [James] went from being a kid in Hauppauge to becoming the first U.S.–born black player in National Hockey League history. His road was a rough one, packed with racism, which is what makes the story so compelling."

— *Newsday*

"The pall racism cast over his career hasn't changed his love for the game itself. Ask James if he'd be willing to go through the whole experience all over again — the taunts, the threats, the tears — and you'll get a simple answer: 'I'd do it again in a heartbeat.'"

— *Vice Sports*

"What surprises so many who don't know James beyond his imposing physique and punishing fists is what a warm, genuine character he is off the ice."

— *ESPN.com*

"He writes honestly about his career as an enforcer — not a goon — whose punching power instilled fear in opponents. He unflinchingly describes the racial abuse he endured"

— ColorOfHockey.com

"Val James is an inspiration on and off the ice."

— @FoxNews

THE VAL JAMES STORY

BLACK

VALMORE JAMES
& JOHN GALLAGHER

ICE

ECW

Published by ECW Press
665 Gerrard Street East
Toronto, ON M4M 1Y2
416-694-3348 / info@ecwpress.com

LIBRARY AND ARCHIVES CANADA
CATALOGUING IN PUBLICATION

James, Valmore, author
Black ice : the Val James story / Valmore James
and John Gallagher. — New edition.

Issued in print and electronic formats.
ISBN 978-1-77041-363-4 (paper)
Also issued as: 978-1-77041-201-9 (bound),
978-1-77090-656-3 (PDF),
978-1-77090-657-0 (ePUB)

1. James, Valmore. 2. Hockey players,
Black—United States—Biography.
3. Black Canadian hockey players—Biography.
4. Hockey players—Biography. I. Gallagher,
John M., author II. Title.

GV848.5.J365A3 2017   796.962092
C2016-906341-0   C2016-906342-9

Editor for the press: Michael Holmes
Cover image: David Madeloni

The publication of *Black Ice* has been generously supported by the Canada Council for the
Arts, which last year invested $153 million to bring the arts to Canadians throughout the
country, and by the Government of Canada through the Canada Book Fund. *Nous remercions
le Conseil des arts du Canada de son soutien. L'an dernier, le Conseil a investi 153 millions de
dollars pour mettre de l'art dans la vie des Canadiennes et des Canadiens de tout le pays. Ce
livre est financé en partie par le gouvernement du Canada.* We also acknowledge the support
of the Ontario Arts Council (OAC), an agency of the Government of Ontario, which last year
funded 1,737 individual artists and 1,095 organizations in 223 communities across Ontario
for a total of $52.1 million, and the contribution of the Government of Ontario through the
Ontario Book Publishing Tax Credit and the Ontario Media Development Corporation.

PRINTED AND BOUND IN CANADA BY FRIESENS   5 4 3 2 1

BLACK ICE

THE VAL JAMES STORY

VAL JAMES

& JOHN GALLAGHER

FROM VJ —

For the love, support, and sacrifice that made possible my impossible dream: I dedicate this book to my parents, Henry and Pernella; to my five siblings, Vernice, Rosemary, Hank, Mary Ann, and Bobby Lee; and to my wife and soul mate, Ina.

With love to Tia, Jasmine, Jordan, and the extended James family; and special thanks to all my teammates for the laughs and the memories.

With deep gratitude to Herb Carnegie, Willie O'Ree, and all those who came before.

FROM JG —

For Deana, Catherine, and Dominick, the loves of my life.

HIS TEAMMATES LOOKED AWAY, pretending not to notice that feared hockey enforcer Valmore James was crying. That the events of recent days would bring tears to his eyes should not have been a surprise. Less than one hour earlier, Val and the Buffalo Sabres had finished playing a fierce road contest against the Bruins at hockey's hallowed Boston Garden. Val had contributed the hard play, and harder punches, that led to his first call up to the National Hockey League.

The years of dreaming and hard work and fighting — especially the fighting — had all brought him to this point. The moment he took to the ice, on a spring evening in 1982, he had become part of a tiny fraternity of American players who made it to the pinnacle of Canada's national pastime. Much more than that, Val James had become the first black American to ever play in the NHL. There had been no ceremony, no public address announcement. But Val knew. And if his dad were still alive, he would have known too.

Still, the tears were not born of the joy of finally making it to the show. Nor were they from the pride of being the first African American to do so. The tears that slipped past his scarred fists were tears of shame. And rage.

Through his tears, Val could see the angry mob that blocked the path of the Buffalo team bus. He saw the spider web splintering of the front windshield, the result of a hurled beer bottle. And he heard the shouted demands of the mob:

"Send out the nigger!"

ONE

SLOWLY, VERY SLOWLY, I lifted my bruised backside off the ice, keeping one eye on the half-dozen entrances to the hockey rink. I knew that Timber, the family dog, was somewhere out there in the empty arena, awaiting his chance to again knock me off my skates. The way I figured, if I could learn to skate despite being repeatedly torpedoed by a burly Doberman pinscher charging out of the darkness, then the checks of opposing hockey players would have no chance of stopping me.

As every new skater quickly learns, I knew that I needed to keep my feet perfectly straight because the slightest shift in my weight would send my skates shooting out in different directions — while my rear end went straight down. And I surely didn't need any help getting there from Timber. Hearing nothing coming from the empty seating area, my attention shifted away from kamikaze canines and back to the task of standing upright on the narrow strips of sharpened steel strapped to my feet.

The leather ice skates were a present from my dad. I wasn't supposed to get them until my birthday, which fell on Valentine's Day, the day that gave me my name (as suggested by my Aunt Maxine), but my old man couldn't wait to see me on the ice so he turned over the skates to me as a Christmas present. Actually, it was even before Christmas, but he knew I had to make up for lost time.

Though not yet 13, I was indeed late getting onto the ice for the first time. Starting younger would have made my stumbles and spills more expected, and less humorous, to onlookers. It would also have meant a shorter falling distance than the six-plus feet that already separated the top of my head from the frozen surface beneath my wobbly feet. There was nothing I could do at this point about the late start, or the countless falls, but at least I was able to collect my beginner bruises in privacy.

By this time, my dad was the operations manager for the Long Island Arena. His jack-of-all-trades position gave him around-the-clock access to its full-sized ice hockey rink. It was here, surrounded only by several thousand empty seats, that I lifted myself off the ice and back onto my skates. Again, and again, and again.

Almost a decade earlier, Henry James had moved our family from Ocala, Florida, to what was then the still sleepy New York City exurb of Suffolk County. Henry and his wife, Pernella, my mom, believed there was more opportunity for their young family in New York than there was in Florida. At that time, during the early days of the Kennedy administration, Ocala was the Deep South and sadly, Jim Crow was still alive and well. My dad's childhood dream of using his considerable football talents to further his education were dashed when my mom became pregnant with me, the first of what would be six children for my folks. In an instant, the pigskin plans of my dad's youth became a lifelong question of what could have been.

With hungry mouths to feed, Henry did not hesitate to use his brawn to bring home a paycheck, but a life up north offered a better opportunity for him to be the last of his line to depend solely on the strength of his back to earn a living. So, he and my mom gathered their few belongings and packed up me and my baby sisters Vernice and Rosemary (Henry Jr., Mary Ann, and Bobby Lee were still just twinkles in my daddy's eye) and off we went.

At the outset, the move to New York changed little more than the weather conditions under which my father toiled. And not for the better. He had traded working in the sugar cane fields and block ice houses of Central Florida for equally hard labor on the farms that still filled vast swaths of Long Island. Everyone in the family had to pitch in, so I had also spent some summer days working in the same fields, alongside migrant workers whose languages I didn't understand and who were gone once the last crop of tomatoes or potatoes were picked. I was 10 years old before our home on Long Island had electricity or running water. That my folks saw this as an improvement over the quality of life they had down south should tell you plenty about how little there was to be had in those days. After a time doing whatever jobs he could find, including picking crops for pennies, my father came to work at the arena.

Like every kid, I grew up believing that my old man had superhuman strength. I would later learn how right I was. Beyond his broad shoulders, my dad was also an excellent mechanic. He could operate and fix any kind of machinery. He was also the hardest-working man I've ever known. He came to the attention of a successful farmer named Ben Kasper. Mr. Kasper owned a farm in Stony Brook and our family moved into a small home on his property. We all pitched in around the farm, and my favorite chores included helping my dad care for the horses.

Besides his farm, Mr. Kasper was also the owner of the Long

Island Arena. He gave my dad a job as a night watchman there. My father soon took over responsibility for all of the physical operations at the building. He cleaned whatever got dirty and fixed whatever got broken. I would soon come to be my father's trusted assistant and the arena would become my second home.

Tonight, with my dad putting out one fire or another in the building, I slid out to the center of the empty ice. I'd grown up watching the Canadian men play hockey for the Long Island Ducks skate on this same ice. I imagined myself as one of them. I could see myself skating quickly up the ice, warding off the bodychecks of opposing defensemen, raising a blizzard of shaved ice as I threw on the brakes, and firing a puck into the net behind the hapless opposing goalie. My folks, no doubt, would be leading the cheers of the crowd. Well, maybe someday. But, for now, I would have to figure out how to shed the folding chair that I was using as a granny walker to steady my balance.

The momentary excitement of getting my skates to coast in the same direction distracted me from noticing the soft padding of feet scrambling up behind me. The James family dog knocked my skates out from beneath me, leaving me, his supposed best friend, lying on my back. I caught a quick glance of Timber the Doberman, seemingly grinning as he beelined back into the darkness of the seating bowl, waiting for his next ambush opportunity.

I could at least take some comfort in knowing that they don't let dogs play ice hockey. So, really, how hard could it be?

TWO

AS I TAUGHT MYSELF TO SKATE, with an eye on joining a youth hockey squad, I also paid greater attention to the pros who practiced their craft at the arena. I could often be found working at my father's side, watching the trademark chaos of the Eastern Hockey League unfold around me.

Professional ice hockey came to Long Island in 1959 when the Rovers, the long-time farm club of the New York Rangers, swapped their Madison Square Garden home in Manhattan for a new one at the Long Island Arena. Foreshadowing the flight of hundreds of thousands of New Yorkers in the coming decades, the Rovers left behind the bustle and diversity of the big city for the rural sparsity and sameness of Long Island's suburbs.

In 1961, the new owners of the Rovers, headed by another Brooklynite-turned-Long-Islander Al Baron, decided they wanted a new, local identity on which natives could build a personal attachment to the team. At the time, the Island was perhaps best known for raising a particularly tasty stock of duck, direct descendants of the famous Peking duck that had been served to Chinese emperors and was introduced onto the Island before the turn of the century. Once here, the American ancestors of these Chinese imports had thrived. Long Island's proud poultry product thus became the namesake for the team's entry in the rough and tumble EHL.

Like the skating Ducks (as opposed to the flying ones), I was also a recent transplant to Long Island, the James family trekking north from Florida around the same time the Ducks were being hatched. I grew up around the team and its players. I worked the Ducks games. My duties included pushing a shovel behind the Zamboni driven by my father to resurface the ice between periods. Myself and other boys performed "go-fer" duties during team practices. Many of the Ducks players became my coaches and mentors. The Ducks provided my introduction to the sport and my model for how the game was meant to be played.

A blank slate when it came to hockey, I absorbed certain lessons watching my hometown squad. To play the game, all you needed was a puck, a stick, and a sheet of ice. For the patrons of the Long Island Arena to more directly join in the fun, they needed nothing more than alcohol. During many a Ducks game, the action on the ice spilled into the stands. And vice versa.

The two far ends of the hockey rink had chain-link fencing to protect the customers from stray — and not so stray — pucks and sticks. Along the side boards, there was no similar barrier between game participants and spectators, with the distinction between the two often becoming blurred. The fans of Long Island loved their Ducks and many of them took personal offense to perceived slights of opposing players, visiting fans, and the always biased referees. More than a few of the Ducks faithful saw their role as only beginning with loud verbal expressions of disapproval. It was a given that paying up to four bucks for a seat entitled you to curse the mothers who had the audacity to give birth to the no-gooders of the opposing team and to bathe those unwelcome visitors in the backwash of your stale beer. Some of these serial beer chuckers left the brew in the can or bottle when pitching it because it was not easy to get loose beer to fly where you wanted it to go. And, with that four bucks already spent, they couldn't afford to waste any more money on errant beer tosses.

One evening, as I took in the finer points of my newly chosen sport, a member of the visiting team's booster club thought turnabout was fair play and delivered an impressively accurate cup of suds to the head of Ducks defenseman John Brophy. Brophy was one of my early hockey mentors, a role he would reprise several times over the nearly 20 years of hockey that lay ahead of me. Brophy was also the ornery, all-time penalty king of the highly combative EHL. Brophy was intense even in practice; I once watched him become infuriated when his French-Canadian teammate Jean-Marie Nicol turned the defenseman inside out with a finesse move. Brophy broke his own stick over the goal post, then Nicol's stick. Not done, he then grabbed a handful of other sticks from the bench and turned them into firewood, too.

In the heat of battle, Brophy wielded his hockey stick like the billy club of a sadistic street cop. The noggins of many EHL veterans — and a fair number of paying fans — bore the permanent, jagged signature of Brophy's wooden massage. Even the referees were not exempt from his physical ire. He had been suspended for the duration of a previous season for manhandling one of the zebras. Al Baron and the Ducks then promptly named the unemployed Brophy as the team's head coach.

Back on the ice this particular evening, Brophy chased the beer tosser through the stands. Now running for his life, the fan fled up the concrete stairs, with Brophy in close pursuit, his skates sparking beneath him. The runner made it out of the building to the parking lot. Brophy followed. Of course, I ran outside to watch the show. I got there in time to see Brophy looking between and under the rows of parked cars, his prey fortunate to have escaped. A change of skates later and Brophy returned to the game at hand.

On the ice, and later behind the bench, John Brophy was nothing less than fearsome. Off the ice, many would be surprised to hear that he could sometimes be a big-hearted softy. As I struggled to learn the game of hockey, my dad recruited another youth player, Greg "Mole" Martinelli, to help me. Mole himself had found hockey through a chance encounter with Brophy. When Mole was about 10, he lived in the Long Island town of Brentwood. During the off-season, Brophy worked laying brick and, this particular summer, he was busy building schools in Brentwood. Mole and some other local kids thought it would be fun to throw dirt bombs at the workers and then run away. It *was* fun, until Brophy caught Mole.

Mole cowered as Brophy growled at him, "Why don't you get a job instead of throwing shit at people who are working?"

"A job?" Mole responded. "But, Mister, I'm only 10 years old."

Brophy told Mole to meet him at the worksite the next day and, when he did, Brophy gave him a case of soda to sell to the workers. During a lunch break, Brophy told Mole that he was a hockey player. Mole didn't know much about hockey, so Brophy told him to tell his parents to bring him to the Long Island Arena for the next Ducks game. He would leave tickets for the family at the will-call window. Mole's folks took him to the game and he got hooked on hockey.

Brophy's opponents may have had trouble picturing this side of him. Frankly, I don't think he would have wanted stories of his decency off the ice to soften his reputation as an on-ice lunatic. Not to worry, I'm quite sure that his reputation for sharp elbows and sharper stick blades remains intact.

Other Ducks games brought more confrontations between players and payers. On-ice fights often continued in the penalty box where the combatants were separated only by a very nervous off-ice official. Opposing teams had to walk a lengthy gauntlet of fans from the ice to the relative safety of the dressing room. One member of the visiting Jersey Devils once took some lumps from a fan who saw nothing unusual about bringing a bull-whip to a hockey game in order to reach out and touch the opposing team. Beer showers were so prevalent that the rival New Haven Blades brought umbrellas to one game. Uniformed police officers were frequently called in to restore peace. I had a front-row seat to the World Wrestling Federation on ice, but without the stage blood. The EHL produced plenty of the real thing. Heroes; villains; colorful team costumes with names such as Ramblers, Rebels, Rockets, and Devils. It was hardly a coincidence that Linda and Vince McMahon owned the Cape Cod franchise of the EHL, years before turning the WWF into a pay-per-view and action-figure empire.

The league was also inspiration for Hollywood's violent hockey classic *Slap Shot*, starring Paul Newman as the player-coach of a failing hockey team that greatly improves its record, and its attendance, by slashing and punching their way past their opponents. The script paid homage to Brophy and the Ducks, amongst many EHL landmarks, borrowing their names and antics for characters in the movie.

With role models like Brophy and his teammates, the Ducks were also an inspiration and influence on my understanding of the sport. All the brawls and everything you saw in *Slap Shot*, I saw watching the Ducks every day. I thought that was the way hockey was supposed to be. Something tells me that many old Ducks fans would still agree with this sentiment.

THREE

FEW THINGS COULD MAKE a 13-year-old hockey player feel more like a big leaguer than a team road trip. I'm talking about trips to far-flung tournaments where long car drives were followed by overnight lodging. As part of the Long Island Ducklings bantam All-Star Team, I participated in a number of these tournaments. One such trip to Michigan stands out, but for the wrong reason.

As usual, hectic work schedules kept my folks from making the trip to Ann Arbor, about 40 miles west of Detroit, so they chipped in their share of the costs and entrusted me to the chaperoning parents of my teammates. By now, I was in the company of boys with whom I would play hockey for the next several years. The hodgepodge of regulars included team captain Richie Campisi, the Amoruso brothers, and the slight but talented goalie, Paul Skidmore. Skidmore's dad, Jim, was Al Baron's partner in ownership of the Long Island Ducks. These guys were good hockey players so we never lacked confidence going against the "cold weather" teams we faced in these tournaments.

For the drive to Michigan, a small caravan of cars was packed tight with as many kids, and as much equipment, as possible.

Similarly, the motel rooms were stuffed with 12- and 13-year-olds, all of us staying up too late and eating too much junk food. And if all of this wasn't enough fun, we also got to play hockey against other traveling teams.

Although I had only been skating a few months, I was a member of the Ducklings All-Star Team. I had a pretty good idea that my place on the team had little to do with my nascent hockey skills. Nor did my size play much of a part in my name being on the roster. Sure, I was a big kid, already nearly six feet tall without skates, and I was showing some of the strength that my old man was known for. I could also skate at a pretty good clip now. But stopping? That was another story. Stopping usually involved running into something. I could get to the puck pretty quick but then, look out: collisions with the boards, with our opponents, and even with my teammates. Sorry about that, boys! So I knew I only made the traveling team because my dad was the ice manager at the Long Island Arena and could get the squad a deal on ice time. The way my dad and I saw it, playing with more skilled players would only make me better. Then, in time, I might actually become an asset, rather than a liability, to the team.

On this Ducklings road trip, we'd won our opening games and earned a spot in the tournament final. Wearing black-and-red jerseys with our team name stitched across the front, my teammates and I skated in the pregame warm-up.

Fans of our opponents taunted us, the despised New Yorkers, with the typical pregame jibes: "Hey, it's the Ugly Ducklings. You guys should be called the Fucklings." Nothing new here, just the same nonsense we had heard before and easily ignored.

As the warm-up drew to a close, each of the teams skated towards our respective benches. I was gathering my thoughts for the upcoming drop of the puck, when I heard someone yelling something that I had not heard before.

"Hey, you, you're nothing but a fuckin' nigger."

I turned to see a young adult, the parent or older sibling of an opposing player. Looking around, I was surprised to see the screamer pointing at me, his face twisted in hate. "I'm talking to you, you nigger. Who told you it was OK for a nigger to play ice hockey?"

Looking back, that was the moment when I truly learned that I was black.

I knew I was black, of course — my skin was darker than all my white neighbors and friends on Long Island. But, up to that point, I had no reason to challenge what my parents told me. I had no reason to think that my skin color made any difference in who I was. This was the first time I learned that being black meant, in the eyes of some people, that I was different, that I was less. I'd never seen this guy before. I've never done anything or said anything to him but, to him, I was a nigger. Something to be mistreated, to be hated.

My teammates led me away and together we vowed to beat our opponents, which we did. The mood in the car was light on the ride home, as it always was when our trip ended in victory. But, this time, I couldn't share in the exhausted joy of my friends. The whole drive back to Long Island, I found that the slur filled my thoughts more so than the trophy that our team was taking home. I never told my father about the incident but I later learned that other parents had. They told Henry James how Valmore and his teammates used the vile attack as motivation to play a strong, winning game. They raved about the kids turning an offensive, negative encounter into something positive. But I just couldn't appreciate the same "happy ending" as the well-meaning parents of my teammates.

While the anger of the stranger was something that was new to me, the level of emotion, the level of hate, that was expressed towards me obviously ran far too deep to be a new feeling for the stranger. If this grown-up from America's heartland hated me without even knowing me, he likely wasn't alone.

My initial surprise and confusion were now mixed with anger. I was angry that I was made to feel different. Different even amongst friends who never gave me any reason to feel that way.

To me, the result of the confrontation in Ann Arbor could only be "happy" if it truly was an "ending." But even then, it just didn't feel that way.

FOUR

AT 14, NOW IN MY SECOND YEAR of organized youth hockey, I was one of the younger players in the midget division. Unlike the bantam traveling team, which capped players at 14 years old, the midgets included players who had not reached their 18th birthday by the start of the season. As a result, there were significant disparities in the size, age, and experience of the players. I was doing fine in the former category, a full six feet tall even if I was still hockey-stick thin at 160 pounds, my bulk not yet able to keep up with my ever-increasing height. However, it was the latter category, hockey experience, where I couldn't make any gains other than continuing to play the game at every opportunity. Improving my skating and puck handling was only part of that experience. At least as important was developing my "sense" of the game, my understanding of the unwritten practices and codes that were largely found outside the rule book and instruction manuals. These intangibles, which were necessary for playing successful hockey, were frequently learned by observing my more seasoned teammates.

The coach of our midget Suffolk Ducks squad was none other than my old man, Henry James. We played our home games at the Long Island Arena. Our road games were held at our opponents' home rinks around the Island and into the outer boroughs of Brooklyn and Queens. There was only a half-dozen or so teams on the schedule so the teams and the players became contemptuously familiar with one another.

Amongst my teammates was Danny Carro. Danny, four years older than me, was a big man. He had several inches on me and outweighed me by at least 50 pounds of muscle. It's hard to believe, but he had an older brother who was even bigger than him. In his own family, Danny may have been the runt of the litter, but compared to the rest of us mere mortals, he was enormous. A fun, playful giant off the ice, Danny was nicknamed "the Strangler" in honor of his favorite professional wrestler. On the ice, Danny was a good player made better by the respect he garnered from foes who knew that any attempt to take liberties with him would be met with an angry, outsized response.

One evening, our Suffolk Ducks played the New Hyde Park Arrows, a team based at Skateland, just over the Queens line into Long Island, and their roster was heavily populated with players from the same area. During the game, in my pursuit of the puck, I arrived at the same time as an Arrows player and we collided against the boards. My opponent was older than me but, while big, he was no bigger than me. As the puck flittered away, the Arrows player made no attempt to chase it and instead he pushed me hard against the boards. I tried to skate past but he cross-checked me with his stick. Then he did it again. Unable to chase the puck, I turned to face this guy. The Arrows player dropped his gloves in what everyone in the rink recognized as the prelude to a fistfight. That is, everyone other than me. I didn't drop my gloves. Instead, I ducked past my challenger and skated away. The game continued and nobody said anything to me about the non-fight.

The following day, Danny and I were working together at the part-time jobs we held at the arena. At lunchtime, as we often did, we set out for a bite. In a scene that never failed to amuse me, Danny struggled to squeeze that enormous mass of meat behind the wheel of his severely undersized Dodge Colt.

On our way to pick up sandwiches at a local deli, we stopped at Danny's nearby house. While I waited, Danny fished through his bedroom closet, coming out with one, then two pairs of boxing gloves. Danny put on one pair and threw the other pair to me.

"Val, you embarrassed yourself yesterday," Danny said. "Worse than that, you embarrassed your father and you embarrassed your team. You're going to learn to fight back right now."

"C'mon, Danny, this is stupid." I had little interest in boxing the monster in front of me, but he was insistent. At the start, I would not fight back so Danny gave me some smacks and body blows. Reluctantly and timidly, I started to hit him back.

"C'mon, you pussy, you can't hit harder than that?" Danny caught me solid on my chin, causing me to bite my tongue. I could taste blood. My mind flashed red and I started pummeling my bigger teammate. Danny sparred for a few moments, but I was pissed and I rained punches down on him. For his own well-being, Danny had to tightly wrap me up in his arms. "Alright, Val, that's enough. You're ready. Enough."

Danny and I did not discuss the training session again and, as luck would have it, the Ducks were next scheduled to play against New Hyde Park in a rematch.

During the early stages of play, my Arrows friend again sought me out, looking to build on the dominance he had asserted in our previous encounter. He again cross-checked me and then squared off in front of me, blocking my path. In an instant my gloves flew from my hands and then, swinging from my feet, my fist exploded square between the eyes of my opponent. Before my gloves had landed on the ice, my challenger was already lying down there, having thrown not a single punch in return. With my fists clenched, I stood ready for a second round but my tormentor remained prone.

On my way to the penalty box, I skated through the congratulations of my teammates and the shocked stares of my opponents. Stopping at the bench, I apologized to my dad. "I'll never embarrass you or our team again." My dad just nodded silently.

Danny smiled at me, shaking his head at the ferocity of what he just witnessed. I shrugged my shoulders and softly joked, "Imagine what I could have done if I had a teacher who knew what he was doing."

In short order, word of the fight passed through the league. In less than a minute, I went from being the intimidated to being the intimidator. I was able to nip any notion that the tall black kid on the Ducks was afraid to stand up for himself. Instead, I had started sowing the seeds of a reputation as someone who was able and willing to exact a cost from anyone who had the misplaced idea that I could be bullied on the ice.

Sadly, Danny Carro would die in a home accident just a few short years after we last played hockey together. He was a cherished friend and childhood mentor. Among the many things I learned from him was how to get respect on the ice. It was really quite simple: If the other team won't give you that respect, then you have to take it. This new attitude immediately translated into more space on the ice to play the puck, for me and my teammates. It was a lesson not found in any training manual.

FIVE

THE LONG ISLAND ARENA was not only the center of our hockey activities, it was the center of our teenage world. For the core group of us, the arena was the primary setting of our adolescent memories. Our gang included hockey players, figure skaters, the offspring of arena and team employees, and the rest of the ragtag group of temporary laborers who helped out around the arena. In many ways, this was our hockey place, our work place, our school, and our clubhouse. And, at the center of all the activities in this building was my father, Henry James.

From the outside, the place looked more like an oversized, tin-roofed barn than a sports and entertainment facility, let alone the biggest such facility that you could find east of New York City at that time. The arena's resemblance to a building you might find on a farm was not completely out of place on Long Island, where the spread of the city's suburbs had only begun to turn the farmland and wooded areas into housing developments. Still, I don't think the arena was purposely built to look like a symbol of Long Island's agricultural history. More likely, it was built in the cheapest manner for getting a roof over 4,000 seats surrounding the main event floor.

The amount of work required of my dad at the arena seemed to be never ending. In addition to running the day-to-day mechanical operations of the arena, my father was responsible for the construction and teardown of the arena floor for the many different types of events held there. From the ice and boards for hockey, to hardwood and hoops for basketball, to stages and floor seating for concerts, to thousands of yards of soil and fencing for the rodeo.

For the most part, it was left to my dad to get these tasks done, and done on time, and, most importantly, done on the cheap. When it came to adult help, Henry James was alone. To get the job completed, he recruited me and a bunch of other local teenagers, most of whom were drawn to the arena to play hockey. Talk about cheap help. Some of us got a few bucks but others of us traded our labor for free ice time. None of us had any money to speak of and the arena kept us busy and, for the most part, out of trouble.

It fell to my dad to herd his teenage crew and keep us on task. He was our boss, but he also worked harder than any one of us. I'm not exaggerating when I say that he regularly worked 20 hours a day. He set an example for those who worked under his supervision. Sure, we worked hard too, but not as hard as Henry. We found time to fit some goofing off into our workday; we were teenagers after all. So, while we worked hard, we also played hard. One of our group christened us "the Scummers," and the name stuck.

The Scummers frequently worked odd hours, which meant that the only kids around for socializing when we finished work late at night would be ourselves. As a result, we spent even more time together and became even closer. One friend recently described our experience as "Lord of the Flies Lite." We had each other and we didn't feel that we were missing out on anything that took place outside our own little community.

When you work with your closest friends, things can get a bit crazy on the job. One example of our mixing of work and play took place during an overnight teardown of one event or another. My brother Hank was too young to be a full-fledged Scummer, but he often helped out around the arena. The work could be tiring but it was much more so when you were humping fences and seats and whatever else needed humping in the middle of the night. On this night, Hank slipped off into the seating bowl of the arena to rest his eyes for a minute or two. Of course, he fell fast asleep. And when my brother Hank fell asleep, nothing could wake him. Well, almost nothing.

One of us had the idea to dress up Hank with whatever accessories had been left behind by that evening's audience. In no time, Hank was snoring away in an old scarf and a trucker's hat. He had an empty booze bottle in his hand and a cigar clenched in his teeth. While we returned to our chores, my father found his snoozing little hobo. It was quickly obvious that we thought the costume was much more amusing than my dad did, who also had some trouble waking my brother. Although he swore he wasn't sleeping, Hank could not explain how he got into the outfit he was wearing. As always, finding ways to laugh made the work pass faster.

Every event scheduled at the arena meant reshaping and reconfiguring the main floor-space. Of course, every event also drew its own unique crowd with its own unique challenges. Every event also had the potential for trouble and troublemakers. Whenever trouble showed its face, Henry put on his bouncer's hat. My father spent more hours at the arena than he did at home. He did not take kindly to fools who looked to cause problems at the arena any more than he would have if they tried to pull the same stunts in our own living room. For many events, watching the crowd became more interesting than watching whatever show was going on.

Chris Brinster, a fellow Scummer and hockey teammate, recently reminded me about one out-of-control brawl that broke out during a concert at the arena. For years, many of the big musical groups that played in New York City would swing out to Commack for another quick payday while they were in the area. Everyone from the Beach Boys to Black Sabbath. The legendary album, *Frampton Comes Alive!*, was recorded at the arena.

We don't recall who the headliner was on this particular night, but we had looked out onto the floor seating-area to see maybe two dozen well-liquored rock fans pummeling each other with fists and chairs. As Chris says, "Henry walked down to the melee. He wasn't one to run. He wasn't that tall either, maybe 5-foot-10, but he was 220 pounds of rock. Henry disappeared into the center of the fight and then, like a Popeye cartoon, bodies began to fly out from the middle of the scrum. A minute later, Henry was standing alone, dusting himself off, and walking back to resume his other duties."

The rock concerts brought some other benefits to the Scummers. During the show, we would catch some of our favorite bands. After the concerts, during cleanup, we would often find "tips" left behind by the paying customers. Full bottles of rum or vodka, maybe an ounce of weed. It's possible that not all of these finds made it into the lost-and-found bin. Some of it might have fueled after-work socializing in the parking lot or maybe at the Commack Drive-In movie theater next door, where we often regrouped to catch a double or triple feature for two bucks a carload. You would be amazed at how many of us could fit into my orange 1972 Pontiac LeMans or, better yet, Tom Hasenzahl's 1963 Cadillac.

One of the more challenging events hosted at the arena was the rodeo. As with any other event, we had to place boards over the ice surface but, with the rodeo, we then had to load tons and tons of soil onto the floor. It was also an adventure every time we had to move the dozens of angry horses and steer into and out of the arena. The rodeo, however, was my dad's favorite event. Out on the Kasper farm, he had really taken to the horses. Like him, they were quiet but powerful.

When the rodeo came to Long Island, my father figured there was no reason he couldn't compete with cowboys from Texas and Oklahoma who were half his age and who had been training their whole lives to ride and lasso. Well, it turns out, my old man was right. Except for one painful ride in which he forgot to take his massive ring of arena keys out of his back pocket before jumping on the back of a bucking bronco, he more than held his own with the hat-and-spur crowd. He had a drawer full of belt buckles that he won in the rodeo competitions. He even held the arena record for the fastest time for roping a calf. I don't think it's a stretch to say that Henry James was the only black cowpoke on Long Island, either then or now.

Another memorable booking was the professional wrestling matches that were frequently held at the arena. Pro wrestling was a favorite amongst the Scummers. We would wrestle amongst ourselves whenever the mood grabbed us, sometimes even when Henry thought we were busy at work. The opportunity to watch our wrestling idols chokehold and body slam each other was always a special treat. Of course, this being the Long Island Arena, the violence was not always confined to the roped-off ring.

On one star-studded wrestling card, there was the always-popular tag team match. One of the legendary tag-teamers wrestling on this particular night called for maintenance assistance when a toilet backed up in the locker room. When my dad arrived, the famous wrestler announced, "At least they sent a nigger to do the nigger work." He quickly learned that Henry James's duties might require him to clean a spilled toilet, but they did not include suffering racist insults, whether or not the slurs came from the mouth of a professional wrestling superstar.

My father lifted the wrestler, who was in full costume, and pinned him against the locker room wall. The wrestler's tasseled boots dangled above the floor. Maintaining his grasp on the struggling 260-pounder with one hand, he pummeled the man in tights with his other hand. The medical staff tried to patch up what was left of the wrestler, who lay moaning where my father had dropped him, in the overflowed toilet waste still on the floor. Being that the blood spilled on that particular night was not the stage blood that the pro wrestler was used to, he was carted off to the local emergency room for more extensive repairs. It was announced over the public address system that the wrestler had taken ill and could not appear. I have purposely withheld the name of this man, who has since passed on, giving his family much more respect than he gave my dad.

To be sure, my father did not look for trouble. However, as Chris Brinster put it, "When he was physically provoked, Henry James was not a man who responded with reason." So, while he did not look for trouble, he was sure to put an end to it when it did pop up. And he ended it quickly. It was a philosophy that I later adopted as I made my way through the hockey ranks.

My dad is gone now. So is the Long Island Arena. It's been

replaced by a Target, the penalty box gone in favor of a big-box store. As we got older, some of us left the Island to play hockey in other states and other countries. In the beginning, we returned each summer, drawn back to the arena where we caught up with old friends and trained together for the next hockey season. Then the years passed and we continued to go our separate ways. As my buddy Tom Hasenzahl recalls, once the arena was torn down, we no longer had that beacon, the central meeting place that had brought us all together. We had come to the arena to learn to play hockey. While there, we also learned the value of hard work, loyalty, and above all, friendship. These were lessons we learned from each other and from a migrant farm worker who wanted a better life for his family.

SIX

IN THE LATE 1960s, word of a new hockey league based in the metropolitan New York area triggered a buzz of excitement amongst the small but crazed group on Long Island who lived and breathed hockey. Emile Francis, the general manager of the New York Rangers, tasked the team's director of player personnel, John Muckler, with forming a junior hockey league to develop 15- to 19-year-old players in the greater New York City area.

Muckler, a former player and coach for the Long Island Ducks, and Lou Vairo, then an air conditioner repairman from Brooklyn, planned out the league's particulars in Muckler's office at Madison Square Garden. Muckler recalls, "Lou spent more time with me than he did with his company." The result was the birth of the Metropolitan Junior Hockey Association, or "the Met League" as we alumni warmly refer to it. Looking back, forming the Met League was only the first time that Muckler would have an impact on my hockey career. I would later learn that his friendship with my dad led to periodic scheming between the two, and phone calls by Muckler to help land me in one training camp or another.

Met League teams were formed in Brooklyn, Manhattan,

Nassau County, Westchester County, New Jersey, and, later, in Suffolk County with the entry of my team, the Suffolk Ducks. We each had our own "home" rink such as the Abe Stark Arena in Coney Island, Skateland in New Hyde Park, and, of course, our home ice, the Long Island Arena.

Muckler was the commissioner of the Metropolitan Junior Hockey Association during the league's first season. When he left New York to take over as the first coach of Minnesota's expansion entry to the NHL, much of the league's operations fell to its co-founder, Vairo, who also coached the Met League's most successful team, the Brooklyn Stars. The Canarsie-born Vairo was a perfect mentor to the hundreds of talented young hockey players in the New York area, who had no guidance or structure beyond the local "little league" organizations in which they had previously played.

Mr. Francis and the Rangers were also terrific "big brothers" to the league and those of us who played in it. As my Suffolk Ducks captain and buddy Greg "Mole" Martinelli points out, "The players didn't have to pay anything to play in the Met League and a lot of these kids didn't have any money to start with. The money for the league came from selling tickets to the game for a buck or two, and the Rangers would fill in the gap with other financial support. The Rangers also loaned the Garden to the Met League for some of our games."

You can imagine the thrill it was for us to play at Madison Square Garden. Back then, the World's Most Famous Arena was a brand new facility, and we were playing some of our games on the same ice that was used by our NHL heroes. On these nights, there might be a couple thousand fans in the stands cheering for us or, if we were playing the local Manhattan team, then we would have a couple thousand fans cheering against us. That was fine too. We were playing on Broadway!

Our coach was former Long Island Ducks player, Sam Gregory. The assistant coach was his former teammate, John Brophy, but Broph would have to bail early in our season once his paying job as a professional player kicked off its own season. Besides our captain, Mole, our team had two excellent goaltenders in Paul Skidmore and Tom Hasenzahl, each of whom would have success playing beyond the Met League, with Skidmore even logging a couple games with the St. Louis Blues of the NHL. As for Hasenzahl, no less than Coach Vairo says that only a freak knee injury kept Hazzie from a successful career in the bigs. Our skaters included two sets of brothers, the Lahjalas and the Amorusos. And when I say "brothers," I mean biological brothers. If it was a brother of color you were looking for, well, you would be stuck with me.

Our team also included the guy who, for my money, was the best player in the Met League: Richie Campisi. He could skate laterally, side to side, better than most players could skate north and south — which is saying something when you consider the talent that played in the Met League in those days.

The level of hockey played in the Met League was impressive. The games were hard fought, combining a high degree of skill with the grit and attitude of New York City. Our opponents included guys like Nick Fotiu, then of New Hyde Park and now a retired Rangers legend. Nicky was older than me, but we hit it off — which, I guess, is better than being hit by him. Actually, while Nicky was one tough hombre, he was not the type to beat up on a younger, less experienced player. It was an early lesson of "the code," the unwritten rules that were followed by the more honorable of those who earned their living with their fists. From those early days, and throughout my career, Nicky always gave me good advice, encouraging me by saying that he thought my hard work would translate into a successful hockey career. He was a gentleman and he made his early bones in the Met League.

Other opponents included the wildly talented Mullen brothers, Tommy and younger brother Joey, of Hell's Kitchen. Of course, Joey went on to score 600 goals in the NHL and his name can be found on both the Stanley Cup and a plaque in the Hockey Hall of Fame. Not too shabby for a kid from the streets of New York.

There was also no shortage of colorful characters in the Met League. Some nights, I might look up and see a goalie stick helicoptering through the air. It was a clear sign that Hazzie, our netminder, was unhappy with a ref's call or the bump of an opposing player. The flying stick was his protest. Another ritual I enjoyed was that of defenseman Bob Yaciuk of the Brooklyn Stars. Bob was bald and to psych himself up before a game, he would break hockey sticks, one after another, over his own cue-ball noggin.

Playing with and against these talented players only made me a better player too. One of my greatest thrills as a young hockey player came when I was named as an alternate to the Met League All-Star Team. Unfortunately, this same memory also brings me sadness, as well as anger. Some of my Ducks teammates, like Mole and Campisi, were also selected for the team but the All-Star Game was not a new experience for them. Nor was it a new experience for our excellent defenseman, Gary Keating. Gary was another fun guy, and he drove one of those small MG sports cars. Tragically, while on his way to one of our games, Gary lost control of his car and he was killed. It was a bittersweet privilege to dress for that All-Star Game as Gary's replacement. I was determined to honor my friend's memory.

The game was played at the World's Fair rink in Flushing Meadow Park, in Queens. My father was there, a rare time that he could peel himself away from his non-stop duties at the Long Island Arena. With my dad watching, I probably played the best game of my young career. Against All-Star competition, I scored a goal, not once, but twice. My father's happy face could have lit up the arena. At 15 years old, I was living a dream.

And then I wasn't.

After my second goal, a smaller but older player, Jack Buckley, skated over to me. He obviously didn't care for my improved play as he bumped me and called me a "jigaboo." Now, I knew the All-Star Game was meant to be a friendly exhibition between players who spend the whole season trying to knock each other on their asses. But Buckley's racist taunt made me see red, and I was not about to let him hide behind the niceties of the day. I dropped him to the ice with one punch. I kept on hitting him until I was pulled off. We were both thrown out of the game because fighting was strictly prohibited in the All-Star Game. Maybe Buckley deserved to be kicked out for his racist trash talk but I'm not sure it was fair to throw him out for fighting, unless that penalty covered his pathetic groveling while getting his ass kicked.

Back in the locker room, I was furious. I was furious at Buckley and I was furious at myself for letting him ruin my great day. More than that, since the players of both teams shared a locker room during this "friendly" competition, that SOB Buckley was sitting across the room from me, licking his wounds. I was slamming lockers and carrying on, thinking that I had embarrassed my father, when the old man walked in. He calmed me down and let me know that not only was there nothing for me to be ashamed of, but he was proud of how I'd played and handled my racist challenger.

Another tremendous honor came to me later that season when my Ducks teammates voted me the inaugural winner of the Gary Keating Memorial Trophy. Gary was a great player and a better friend. For my Met League teammates to present me with an award in Gary's name was one of the highlights of my hockey career.

Sadly, the Met League lasted for only a handful of seasons. As we understood it, the newly formed Islanders franchise told the Rangers that they wanted to take over the league. The Islanders lacked the same commitment of time and money, so the Met League, as we knew it, went out of existence. But not before giving me and the other players a taste of what it was like to play truly organized hockey. A good number of us were able to build on the skills and exposure that we got playing in the Met League and graduate to more advanced levels of hockey. Without the Met League, we wouldn't have gotten that opportunity.

Coach Vairo also did well for himself after helping put together the Met League. After organizing and growing hockey in his hometown, he did the same on a national level. Lou went on to mentor young hockey players from all over the country as a major player in the USA Hockey Program. He also coached the United States hockey team at a number of international tournaments, including the 1984 and 2002 Olympics. Again, not too bad for a bunch of New Yorkers who loved hockey.

SEVEN

BY THE TIME I was in my mid teens, my family had moved from Stony Brook to Hauppauge. Hauppauge was no closer to Commack and the Long Island Arena than Stony Brook, but it was worlds closer to the vision my folks had for a better life when they moved our family from Florida to New York. Living in this working-class neighborhood, my folks must have thought we had finally arrived. Behind us for good was the one-room share-cropper's house with neither electricity nor running water. Also in the rearview mirror were the long, hot days they spent picking crops. To be sure, my parents still worked hard, but they had finally moved beyond life as migrants traveling with the season to find their next paycheck.

While our modest home in Hauppauge represented the Long Island of my parents' dreams, their own upbringing in the South had a major influence on how we were raised. My folks had come a long way from Ocala, but plenty of southern traditions had hitched a ride on their trip up to New York.

While my dad worked endless hours at the arena, my mom, Pernella, took care of the house and the six of us kids. As hard as my old man worked, I don't think my mom had it any easier with our full house. I was the oldest of three boys and three girls. When time allowed, nothing recharged my mom's battery like the time she spent fishing. From her youth, she loved to fish. She and I would often go to Lake Ronkonkoma where I would row the two of us around the lake for hours. My mom was not a petite woman, and I'm convinced that the time I spent rowing that boat helped me develop my upper body strength.

My mom was a master fisherman, as good as any I've ever seen. Making her success even more remarkable was that she fished using nothing more than a 10-foot bamboo pole with a hooked line tied to the far end. She didn't use a reel as a little girl in Florida in the 1940s and 1950s. So she didn't use one as a mother of six on Long Island in the 1960s and 1970s. To keep a ready supply of bamboo poles, she told all visitors from down South to pack an extra pole or two on their trips to New York.

Out on the lake, we never failed to draw the attention of the other fishermen with their fancy rods and reels. They would smirk at us as we set out. Then their jaws would drop when my mom came back to shore with her catch. Her five-gallon pail was always overflowing with fish, including sunnies, perch, and rainbow trout. I saw her catch 10-pound bass with nothing more than an earthworm on the end of that bamboo pole.

My favorite part of the day came when we headed back to Hauppauge with my mom's catch so she could "do them up right." I always worked up a good appetite rowing that boat, and arriving home meant the payoff was only minutes away. She would gut and clean the fish, her knife slicing and filleting with an ease that came from decades of repeating that same task. The fillets were then thickly battered in flour, corn meal, salt, pepper, and other spices, using a secret recipe that the mothers of our family passed down through the generations. The battered fish was then golden-fried in an open pan, the smells filling my mouth with water. That batter could put 10 pounds on you in a flash. But it was intoxicating. It melted in your mouth and once you started, you just couldn't stop eating.

Fishing was only one of the traditions my mother brought with her to Long Island. In the way of the South, she told us stories about the history of our family and how one generation built upon another. It was probably inevitable that some of her southern spirituality would rub off on me. One of my own chapters in our family folklore was written before we moved to Hauppauge. I was maybe 10 years old at the time and we still lived in the one-room house on the farm in Stony Brook. I was outside the house, playing alone with the 10 or 12 marbles that made up all of the toys I owned at the time. I glanced up and saw a stranger walking down the dirt road, still the most of a mile away from the house. I looked away for only a couple moments, just long enough to shoot two or three marbles through the dust. When I looked back up, the man was only about 30 feet away. He was an older black man with thick, kinky hair — what my mom called "Negro hair" — that could snap a comb. He was wearing a brown corduroy overcoat and he had a perfect smile of straight white teeth. He just stood there and smiled at me without saying a word. I was scared and I quickly gathered up my marbles so I could rush to the safety of our home. When I got to my feet, the man was nowhere to be seen. I hurried into the house and told my mother what just happened.

"Oh, that was your grandfather, Valmore." My mother told me that I had just described her father. "He must have come to see you." She went on to explain that I hadn't recognized him because he had died in Florida, long before I was born. My mom had found nothing unusual about the visit of my late grandfather, so neither did I.

Our family's southern traditions continued to be part of our life once we moved to Hauppauge but, as we got older, those traditions competed with the ways of our friends and our adopted home of Long Island. While my mom's "old school" brand of fishing was a product of her southern upbringing, the same certainly could not be said about my dad's love of ice hockey. That was learned on Long Island. He passed that passion on to me and, in my last year on the Island, I was playing hockey for both the Met League and Hauppauge High School.

Ice hockey was a brand new sport at Hauppauge High School, but we had some terrific players in our district. My teammates, who were also my classmates, included my friend and neighbor Chris Brinster, who later played professional hockey in Europe, along with Richie Campisi, Paul Skidmore, and Steve Amoruso, each of these last three earning Division I college scholarships along the way. Our coach was none other than Henry James, my dad. Henry never played ice hockey and he never skated a day in his life, so he ran our drills while wearing his work boots. When we were short a goalie in practice, he filled in as netminder by playing on his knees. By the time practice was finished, he was covered in welts.

I can only think of one time that my old man's coaching duties were affected by the fact that he was my dad. In one home game that we played against Commack High, I got into a scrum with a Commack player in front of their bench. A grown-up on the bench reached over the boards and started pushing and pulling on me. This guy was enormous, certainly north of 300 pounds.

My dad was at our bench, in a suit and tie, when I skated over. "Hold on one second, boys," he said. He called for a time-out and began walking around the interior of the arena. The grown-up on the other team saw Henry and came walking around to meet up with him. As they approached one another, my dad hit the guy and he just disappeared out of view into the arena hallway. My dad followed him out of sight and then, a minute later, my dad walked out by myself. He walked all the way back around the arena and returned to our team bench. Fixing his tie, he said, "OK, boys, let's get back to work."

I only played for Hauppauge that first year, but it was a great way for our school to kick off its hockey program. We won every game and swept the championship of the Suffolk County High School Hockey League.

Although I was only 16 years old at the end of that hockey season, my days in Hauppauge, and on Long Island, were counting down. I wanted to continue to develop my hockey skills. New York had given me a firm foundation, both at home and on the ice, but it was now time for me to take the values and lessons I had learned and apply them in a world far removed from my Long Island home. Just as my parents had looked to the north in search of their dreams, I now looked in the same direction, towards Canada, to chase my own.

EIGHT

MY PATH FROM LONG ISLAND to Canada in the mid-1970s was set in motion a decade earlier by a hockey player who had taken the exact opposite route. In the mid-1960s, John Muckler had graduated from being a defenseman on the Long Island Ducks to being the team's coach and general manager. On a visit to his hometown of Midland, Ontario, Muckler's Uncle Irv told him about an undiscovered local hockey talent. Uncle Irv had been operating the hockey rink in Midland, and he was impressed by the play of Bernard "Buzz" Deschamps. On his uncle's word, Muckler invited Buzz down to Long Island. Buzz went on to be perhaps the best hockey player in the history of the Ducks franchise. In the 1963–64 season, Buzz scored a team record 57 goals.

After retiring from the game, Buzz settled on Long Island where he helped spread the sport of ice hockey. Amongst his many mentoring roles were the years he spent coaching young players, from mites to the college ranks, the latter as coach of the men's teams at St. John's University and Stony Brook University.

By the time I was 16, Buzz was confident that I and a number of my Met League teammates were ready to step up to Canadian competition. While hockey was new to Long Island, it was the national pastime in Canada. If we wanted to test our game, and to improve, we would have to go north, where the sport was born and where many youngsters take to the ice soon after taking their first steps.

One of Buzz's friends back in Midland was Ron Sauvé, the owner and manager of the Midland Flyers, a new entry in the Ontario Hockey Association. The team competed at the Junior B level, a training ground where young players battled for the opportunity to move on to Junior A, a higher level of organized amateur hockey. Particularly at that time, the typical path to bigger and better leagues came through these junior ranks.

Buzz told Sauvé that he had four kids from Long Island that he wanted to get into the Midland training camp. Sauvé responded, "Four Americans? They'll run me out of town!"

Sauvé had good reason for his concern. Like in the rest of the country, hockey was a religion in Midland. It was a place where there was nearly an uprising in the streets when the town looked to raise the hourly ice rental price by two bucks. Buzz assured Sauvé that the players he was recommending were all good hockey players and good kids. Risking the wrath of his towns-folk, Sauvé gave in to his old friend's request and agreed to let us come to training camp. In any event, as Sauvé told Buzz, "your Americans will never beat out our Canadian kids anyway."

My dad was a much easier sell than my mom on the idea of allowing their eldest to leave high school and head off to Canada to play hockey. As my old man again told me, "you will never know how far you can go unless you give it your best shot." He had given up whatever chance he had at a football scholarship when I showed up in my mom's belly. He never said as much, but I suspect he carried a pile of "what ifs" with him throughout his life and he didn't want to see me weighed down with the same questions. Of course, there were no guarantees of success accompanying me on my trip to Canada but, as my dad well knew, not going only guaranteed that my hockey dreams would certainly go nowhere.

With the blessing of my folks, I packed my bags for what I hoped would be a yearlong trip. Along with my friends Tom Hasenzahl, Richie Campisi, and Steve Amoruso, we squeezed into Buzz's station wagon with our equipment and our dreams of hockey glory.

Midland is about two hours north of Toronto. It is known as the "gateway area" to Ontario's cottage community, where many Canadians vacation when the ice finally does melt. But we were not going there during the summer to boat or fish. We were going there for the long, cold hockey season.

Right from the start, it was obvious that we weren't welcome in Midland. Our own teammates had as much love for the new kids from the States as did our opponents and their fans, which was none. We had two-a-day practices and our Canadian teammates took every opportunity to try to prove that we didn't belong.

Besides the Long Island Four, there was another American on the training camp roster, a kid named Malone from Boston. He came into the locker room after one practice to find that the Canadians had piled all of his equipment in the center of the room and had taken turns pissing on it. Malone could barely hold back his tears as he gathered up his stuff. He left the locker room and went home to Boston, never to return. If the natives had similar plans for the rest of us, I have to give my friend Tom Hasenzahl much of the credit for changing their minds.

Hazzie was an excellent goalie but, like many who played that position, he was also a madman. In general, I think you have to be a bit nuts to purposely throw yourself in front of hard rubber pucks traveling at close to 100 miles per hour. That was Hazzie. He was six feet and five inches of fearless fury. If he felt that a player was shooting high on him, he would shoot the puck back at the player's head. He fiercely guarded his space in front of the net. If you backed in too close to his crease, you would soon be wishing you had your shin pads on backwards.

During team practices, Hazzie fought almost every single day with our own guys. In no time, he was playing with a broken nose and two black eyes. But he still never gave an inch. The Canadians thought it would be good, clean hazing fun to hold down Hazzie and cut his long hair. Hazzie broke his stick over a bathroom stall and promised to impale the first would-be barber to take a step in his direction. Needless to say, he kept his long locks.

The tide began to turn in one early pre-season game we played on the road against Orillia. Three of their guys jumped our captain. He was getting his ass kicked pretty good and the other skaters we had on the ice, all Canadians, just stood around and watched the show. Hazzie, in net, was the only American on the ice. Seeing that his captain could use a hand, he flew out of the crease and jumped into the brawl. The fight went on for a good five minutes. When it was over, Hazzie and our captain were a mess. Their jerseys and pads were torn off, they were bloodied up, and they were naked from the waist up.

We went into the locker room between periods and I sat with Hazzie. We were laughing about what a mess he was when our coach came in. Our coach was Mike Dubeau, a retired player and former tough guy who had been Bobby Orr's defense partner when they played for the Oshawa Generals. He was furious.

Coach Dubeau kicked a hockey glove across the room and it knocked over a shelf of equipment. He lit into the team. "The next time my rookie goalie has to protect my captain, I'll cut this whole fuckin' team."

When we returned to the ice, it was my turn. One of the Orillia players called me a "nigger." It was my first game for Midland, and the first time I would have that slur hurled at me north of the border. I lost it.

"I just leaned against my net and watched Valmore pummeling the shit out of this guy," Hazzie says. "Valmore was a guy who kept his cool a long time, but once he got mad — truly mad — it became a dangerous situation. Valmore was just hammering this big mouth and the officials looked like they were going to shit themselves. They were afraid to break it up because they had no interest in getting hit with one of his punches."

Hazzie was right about my temperament. I was pretty good at keeping my emotions in check. However, there were two things that could send me over the edge. If my opponent tagged me with a good punch, that would piss me off. Fortunately, that didn't happen all too often. The second thing that could trigger a furious response was having an opponent curse me with racial slurs. We might have been wearing different jerseys, but I liked to believe that, as members of the same hockey fraternity, there was a certain level of respect, even amongst opponents. Calling me a nigger was beyond insulting to me, and to my family. Words like that cut me worse than any punch. When I was verbally assaulted in that way, all bets were off — as my mouthy friend in Orillia learned that night. It appeared that his teammates also took note of what the consequences would be, as they kept their mouths shut the rest of the way. Unfortunately, their fans picked up the slack. The slurs rained down on me from the crowd. At one point, Hazzie smashed his stick against the glass to get the attention of one group of racists.

After the game, our Canadian teammates took us American boys out for a nice old-fashioned bender. We got good and shit-faced. In those 60 minutes, we had become a team. Every one of the Long Island kids made the Midland squad. Coach Dubeau caught a ton of flack for keeping us, but he looked at us as part of what he was putting together in Midland.

After the battle in Orillia, the bond with our Canadian counterparts grew stronger every day. Our home fans were quick to warm up to us too. Since ours was a new team in the league, not a lot was expected of us. But we made it exciting. Our beautiful 100-year-old Midland Arena was filled to capacity with thousands of fans cheering us on most every game. Thousands more listened to Tom Shields's play-by-play on CKMP 1230 AM. We had a loyal booster club that traveled by bus to our away games. A late-season run resulted in us clinching a playoff spot, a result beyond Midland's wildest dreams. Under Coach Dubeau, we won more on effort and teamwork than talent, and the fans responded. They appreciated our hard work and, at least in Midland, us Yanks were accepted as one of their own.

Unfortunately, things away from Midland were a different situation altogether. I faced much more racial heckling and cursing on the road in Ontario than I ever did back home in New York.

When the slurs came from our opponents around Ontario, it usually only happened one time for each team. By speaking to me that way, you were telling me there was no limit to the hurt you were willing to put on me. So I had no problem responding in kind. Still, there was little I could do when their home crowds got in on the act. I tried not to acknowledge their hatred and instead tried to remain focused on my game. Most times, I think I fooled them into thinking that their chants and catcalls didn't bother me. But of course they did. I was 16, I was 600 miles from home, and scores of strangers were calling me a nigger. Since I couldn't punch out the whole crowd, I stepped up my physical play against their boys on the ice.

While the instances of racism I faced while playing in New York were rare, I wonder if that left me underprepared for what I faced during those early days in Canada. Would more racism earlier have thickened my skin and made me stronger in the face of what was to come? It's a hell of a thing when you have to wonder if you would have been better off if you had been called "nigger" more often when you were growing up.

My friend Greg Martinelli said that I was different, older, when I came back to Long Island from Midland after that first season. "When Valmore left less than a year earlier, he was just another kid. He was hardworking but, like other kids, he would be joking around and trying to hide from his father, maybe sneak a nap in the locker room. When he came back at the end of the season, it was incredible how much he had grown and matured. He now had a more serious side. He really did come back as an adult."

Ten years after Buzz Deschamps was recommended to John Muckler by his Uncle Irv, the pipeline of hockey talent between Midland in Canada and Long Island in the States no longer ran in just one direction. I went to Canada to work on my game. I became a better player. But for the first time, I was also forced to confront that to some, no matter how well I played, no matter what I did in my life, I would always be a nigger.

NINE

THE STRUGGLE TO PROVE that we could succeed in Midland — in Canada — was not only waged on the ice. When I arrived in Canada as a 16-year-old, it was the first time I was away from my family and my home on Long Island for any extended period of time. From the beginning, my emotions swung wildly between the excitement over my new freedom and the sadness that came with being so far from home. Of course, there was no internet or cellphones, so our communication with home was limited to writing letters and the very occasional phone call. We would leave Long Island at the end of the summer, return briefly at Christmas, and then come back home again at the end of the hockey season. Any kid our age would get homesick over the separation, but I felt, for the first time, an extra level of anxiety based on the color of my skin.

After the initial resistance to the American players coming in to "steal" roster spots from the local boys, the people of Midland came to welcome me warmly. They opened their homes, quite literally, as local families put us up as borders during the season. I attended the local Midland Secondary School. In many respects, the folks of Midland treated me as one of their own, just as they did all the teenage hockey players who came to town. Still, there was no getting over the fact that I was different, even more different than the other young strangers who came to play hockey.

Since there were four of us who came to Midland from Long Island, I was fortunate to have some of my friends along with me on this journey. Tom, Richie, and I were placed together with our first billet family. It didn't take long for us to screw up. As soon as there were no adults around, we had a party. We thought we cleaned up pretty sufficiently, but the smell of booze rose up out of the pores of the house once the heat was turned on. One strike and we were out.

Richie and I were moved in with the family of Ron Sauvé, the team manager. But we didn't get off that easy. Ron sat us down and made us drink beer. It hardly seemed like a punishment — at the start. Then he had us drink some more, one after another, until we got sick. Ron woke us up first thing the next morning to go to practice, our stomachs twisting and our heads pounding. It seems strange now that kids were punished like that back then. It was pretty common in those days. If you caught a kid smoking, you would make him inhale three packs of cigarettes until he puked on himself. You can't do that nowadays. That's probably a good thing.

I would like to say that Ron's lesson set us on the straight path, but memories are short when you're 16. Ron had us go to bed at a certain time each night. We often said our goodnights and then slipped right out to party. Ron would peek in later to check on us. Seeing figures lying under the bunched-up covers and our shoes under the bed, we always passed bed check. Well, almost always.

We didn't get in too much trouble when we snuck out after

47

curfew. Just typical teenage nonsense. One night, after quenching our thirsts, we set out to rearrange a massive stone fountain in the neighboring town of Wasaga Beach. We lifted these enormous stones and rearranged them a short distance away. We didn't break anything, we just moved, by hand, stones that had been placed using heavy machinery. Coach Dubeau came into practice the next morning and said that he had been asked by the authorities whether he thought any of his players were involved in the prank. "Of course, I told them that my guys would never be involved in something so juvenile." Looking back, we could have done worse things.

The Sauvé's old farmhouse became our home too. Their daughter Judy, my "billet sister," remembers it exactly right. "Val was a part of our family. He and Richie Campisi and the other hockey players lived with us from September until June. They ate dinner with us. They celebrated holidays with us. They were like another member of the family. My mom cooked their meals for them and cleaned their clothes. They had the same rules as the rest of us. When they broke the rules, they were punished. I remember Val and the boys sneaking out of the house. They were little buggers. My dad was a tough guy and it took a lot of guts to sneak out of his house. When they got caught, my dad made sure that they paid for it at practice. They would have the toughest practices of their lives after they were caught . . . My dad could be strict but he became very fond of Val."

In all ways, I was involved in the same activities and hijinks as the other visiting hockey players and I was treated as well as each of them, whether or not we deserved such good treatment. I was never made to feel different but it was still difficult for me not to feel that way. Even my homesickness felt different to me. Through no fault of anyone in Midland, the feeling of loneliness was more intense in my case. I had come from a place where there were very few black people. But there were some, like George Horton, a fellow hockey player on the Long Island circuit, and, of course, there was always my family. Back home, at the end of every day, I was able to look in the faces of people who looked like me, people who understood my experiences because they had also lived them.

In this new place, there was no one who looked like me. No one on the team, no one in the school, and no one I saw in town. No black people whatsoever. Except me. Even though Midland allowed me to fit in, I couldn't help but stand out. Our team broadcaster Tom Shields points out, "When Val came to Midland, there was an aura about him because of his size and because he was American but, mostly, because he was black. A lot of people were first drawn to him because they hadn't seen a black player before. Back then, we used the term 'colored' to describe black people, and that was how we described Val, even on the radio."

Of course, when I was subjected to racial abuse on road trips, I could count on the support of my teammates. They always said the right things but, try as they may, they couldn't really sympathize with what I was going through. An old Midland teammate recently brought up an incident when opposing fans threw bananas at me. What the hell could my fellow teenagers on the Flyers ever say to make that better? They would be offended on my behalf but, not being black themselves, they just could not relate to the pain and humiliation and anger that I was experiencing. In that sense, I was very much alone.

When I first heard that some jackass in London, Ontario, threw a banana at Wayne Simmonds of the Philadelphia Flyers in

September 2011, I thought, *Wow, they're still at it, huh?* It brought me back to the days when I dealt with the same garbage. Even more recently, Joel Ward of the Washington Capitals lived out every young hockey player's dream, scoring an overtime goal in Game 7 of a playoff series against the Boston Bruins. Some courageous Boston fans tried to ruin the moment by going online and flinging racial filth at Ward from the safety of their computers. On the positive side, when these attacks happen now, everyone knows about it and people come forward to condemn it. Back in my day, it happened much more often and it certainly wasn't front page news when it did. Still, it's a shame that a guy like Ward would even have to answer questions about what some idiots said about him on the biggest day of his career.

The insults and slurs made the distance between me and my family seem even greater than the hundreds of miles that already separated us. Of course, I was free to leave Canada and return home at any time. But I was determined to play hockey. Even if that meant spending a good chunk of my adolescence away from my family, surrounded by friends, but still alone.

TEN

AFTER TWO YEARS OF JUNIOR B in Midland, I was eager to take a shot at Junior A. I had developed a reputation in Ontario as a player who was willing to go hard into the corners, a place of big bodies and sharp elbows, in order to dig out a loose puck. I was also known to be more than willing to drop an opponent who tried to take cheap shots at my teammates.

My reputation caught the attention of Muzz MacPherson, the coach of the Sault Ste. Marie Greyhounds, a Junior A team in the Ontario Hockey Association. Sault Ste. Marie had a long history of graduating players to the pro ranks. Muzz had received a good report from my coaches in Midland and he drafted me to play for the Greyhounds. This was a big honor but it also caused a dilemma. The Junior A Quebec Remparts of the Quebec Hockey League had invited me to camp as well. The coach of the Remparts was my dad's friend, Ron Racette.

I had met Ron earlier that year when he coached the Long Island Cougars, which was the farm team of the Chicago Cougars of the WHA. After the Ducks folded, following the 1972–73 season, the Cougars played the next two years at the Long Island Arena. These would be the last two years in which the arena would host professional hockey. After John Brophy coached the first year, Ron coached the Cougars during the team's final season. During that time, Ron had become friendly with my dad. Beyond being a good coach, Ron was also a good sport. He had to be during his time on Long Island.

Prior to the start of a Cougars home game against the Philadelphia Firebirds, my dad accidentally totaled one of the goal nets while driving the Zamboni. When 20 minutes of pounding with a sledgehammer did little to restore the goal to shape, Ron and the Firebirds' coach agreed that the teams would switch ends every 10 minutes, thus sharing the indignity of protecting the mangled goal.

During another Cougars home game, several players collided with the Zamboni door. The door was always creaky and rickety, so my dad had propped it into place with a hockey puck. When the players went into the boards chasing the game puck, the second puck also popped out. For half a minute, the players were chasing two different pucks.

Despite the unconventional twists that always seemed to accompany hockey at the Long Island Arena, Ron and my dad became friends.

During the Christmas break of my last year in Midland, my dad asked Ron if I could skate with the Cougars during their practices. Although I was a teenager, Ron agreed to my old man's request. "He can skate with us, Henry," Ron told my dad, "but don't complain to me if he gets flattened out there." My dad wasn't too worried about me. Of course, his advice for my first practice with professional hockey players included the expected tip to protect myself and keep my head up, but he also reminded me, "And, for Christ's sake, don't hurt Ron's guys. This is their livelihood!"

I did take some good licks in those practice sessions but I also felt that, for the most part, I gave as good as I got. Ron must have agreed because he invited me to try out for the Remparts.

I was excited to accept Ron's offer because of our prior relationship and because a number of my friends were headed to the same camp, including my fellow Long Islander Chris Brinster. I called Muzz and told him of my connection with Ron and asked if he would object to me going to the Remparts camp. Muzz was not impressed with my invitation to play in the QHL, the hated rival of the OHA. Instead, he tore into me. "If you aren't at the opening of our camp, I will make damn sure that you never play in Ontario again as long as you live." Despite Muzz's my-way-or-the-highway invitation, my dad and I decided that being black-listed by a well-connected hockey man like Muzz was probably not going to be helpful to my career. So I packed up and set off alone for Sault Ste. Marie. I was still going to have the chance to play hockey and I planned to make the most of it, looking forward to the opportunity to meet the new owner of the Greyhounds, none other than hockey great Phil Esposito! I would also meet a baby-faced Ted Nolan, a fellow player at that camp and someone with whom I would have the pleasure of reacquainting in the coming years.

I worked hard in the Sault Ste. Marie camp, and I must have caught Muzz's attention because he had me suit up for an exhibition game against the Sudbury Wolves. The talk was that the best fighter in the OHA played for Sudbury. Buzz put me on the ice opposite this guy. He was two years my senior but, when we dropped our gloves, I beat him soundly. After the game, Muzz called me into his office and congratulated me on making the team. I was thrilled at this major accomplishment. I was able to make a rare phone call home that night and my dad could not have been more proud of me. When I hung up, I had no doubt that he was lighting up the phone lines, sharing the good news. For my part, I slept 10 feet above the mattress that night. However, the celebration lasted only 15 hours.

The following morning, Sault Ste. Marie made a trade that left them with an extra body on their roster. I was cut less than one day into my Greyhounds career. I had to call my dad with the bad news. I caught a flight back to Long Island and my old man was waiting for me at the airport. As we sped down the Southern State Parkway towards our Hauppauge home, it was obvious from his interrogation that he was peeved. I explained how things went down with Muzz, but I could tell he was carefully dissecting my story, making sure that I wasn't the cause of my premature return home. Thankfully, I was able to satisfy Judge Henry!

The next morning I had a 3 a.m. wake-up call for a 6:30 flight to Quebec City. I was very fortunate that Ron Racette was still willing to let me join the Remparts camp. I still had a chance to play major junior hockey after all, no thanks to Muzz MacPherson.

Coming over from Ontario, I was the last arrival to the Remparts camp. Unfortunately, I still arrived in Quebec City in time for the physical exams that were being performed by the team doctor. It started with the typical stuff. The doctor checked your height, weight, heart rate, and the always popular "turn your head and cough." The Remparts also employed a pain threshold test that I had never seen before. The test involved taking the spikes from the bottom of football cleats, placing the pointed side of the cleat on the cartilage alongside the player's shin bone, and wrapping a blood pressure cuff over the cleat. Then the fun really began. The doctor pumped up the cuff, tighter and tighter, until the player could take no more. It hurt like hell and the players were screaming their heads off. I just bit down hard and let them pump away. The doctor cried "uncle" before I did. I felt I could go further, but he stopped because he was afraid that the cleat might pierce my cartilage.

I also wasn't late enough to avoid my rookie initiation. My new teammates seemed like a great group of guys and they welcomed me with open arms. Of course, I have to think that part of the reason that they were happy to see me was because I was new meat, another new guy they could haze. They wasted little time in giving me my first French-Canadian haircut. To be more accurate, they shaved my head. To be even more accurate, they kind of shaved my head. Instead of taking it all off, they shaved only the sides, leaving me with the most cock-eyed Mohawk you've ever seen. My roommate at the time was my old buddy Chris Brinster. He'd probably disagree, but I think Chris's haircut was even worse than mine. His shave job was spotted with a few ugly patches of hair that clung to his scalp like a family of hungry mice.

Like all the young players, Chris and I were put up by a local family. Our billet family stuck us on a pair of cots thrown down in the basement. And that was before they saw our haircuts. The two of us just sat on our cots, pointing at each other and laughing our asses off. We had to let the haircuts grow out on their own, so we wore hats in public. Of course, our teammates would wait until we were trying to chat up some of the local gals before snatching our hats away.

Our new teammates were also always willing to help us out with the language of our new city. They would offer us helpful French phrases meant to say things like, "may I have a cup of coffee" or "thank you." It wasn't long before we learned that the phrases actually meant "eat shit" or "get fucked." Fortunately, the locals were wise to the rookie initiations and we didn't offend too many people.

It didn't take long for me to realize that getting cut by Muzz was really a blessing in disguise. Quebec City was a big, cosmopolitan city. It had about 50 times the population of my last hockey home of Midland. I soon came to learn that there are few things better in this world than to be a hockey player for the home team in a beautiful, hockey-crazed town. Especially when you were winning.

ELEVEN

SINCE ONLY THE BETTER Junior B players were picked to play Junior A, the level of hockey played in the Quebec Hockey League was a considerable step up from what we'd played in Midland. On any given night in the Q, you might look up and find yourself standing across from someone like a young Mike Bossy, who played for Laval. Mike had the best wrist shot I ever saw, but his slap shot was even better. Just vicious. Mike was always very friendly to me but I suspect that was because I had 40 pounds of muscle on him back then and he was petrified that I was going to destroy him. Little did Mike know, he made me plenty nervous too. I didn't want to get hit with that slap shot of his. So Mike and I worked out an understanding. "Listen, Mike, I won't run you, but if you're going to wind up for a slapper, let me know. I'll be the swinging gate getting out of your way."

Not only were the players faster and more skilled in the Q, they were also bigger, stronger, and tougher. Everyone was trying to prove they could play at this level and beyond. This was the best opportunity to convince the scouts that you were worthy of an NHL team risking one of its precious draft picks. Everyone wanted to show they were the best puck handler or the most impenetrable defenseman or the baddest man when the gloves were off. I was no different in wanting to make my mark.

Upon my arrival in Quebec City, Coach Racette introduced me to some of my new teammates. He told them that he didn't think our team was tough enough. The guys were getting pushed around, which meant the team couldn't play winning hockey. Ron told them that we were going to begin pushing back, starting with me.

Hockey is a beautiful, graceful sport, but it is also a contact sport. The game could be plenty rough at times. This was certainly the case in Quebec. Not everyone on the team liked the idea of being more physical. In the minds of some, the more we hit our opponents, the more they would hit us. I couldn't believe my ears. Although I was brand new, I reminded them that they were already getting clobbered. And, without any consequences, they were going to keep on getting clobbered. There was a little more whining so I said, "If you're that scared, just stay in the locker room. The rest of us will do what we need to do to protect ourselves, and to win some hockey games too."

A couple of my old teammates recently reminded me of my own introduction to the intensity of the games played in the QHL. As Chris Brinster recalls, "In Val's first exhibition game for Quebec, the Remparts were playing the Cornwall Royals, in Cornwall. Their rink was an old barn with ice only 160 feet long, instead of the standard 200 feet. The Royals had twin brothers, the Bardens, who were supposed to be the toughest players in the QHL. In the first period, Val was on left wing and he had just gathered in the puck when one of the Bardens slammed into him, dropped his gloves and punched Val three straight times in the head. Val looked at him, shook his head, and punched the shit out of Barden. The guy couldn't throw another punch. Right from that beating, word of Val's fighting ability spread throughout the league."

I wound up dismantling the second Barden later that night, but what I remember most was the gradual buy-in of my new team. In the first period, some of my teammates cringed as I hit everything in my sight. They thought I was going to get them killed. Later, after I busted up the second twin, I slowed down as I passed our silent bench on my way to the penalty box. "Well, boys, there's another guy who won't be bothering you tonight so how about showing some support." Led by Coach Racette, our bench exploded in cheers. Ron's plan for stiffening our team backbone was underway. Oh yeah, I also got on the score sheet that night, netting my first goal as a Rempart, putting a slapper past future NHL goalie, and my future teammate, Tim Bernhardt.

Another Remparts teammate who I would go on to play with for years was Pierre Legace. Pierre was an excellent hockey player and tough as hell. We played together in Quebec and Erie, spending many of those years as housemates as well as teammates. When we first met, I didn't speak any French and he didn't speak any English so we helped teach our language to each other. And not just the curse words.

Pierre was there during my first days in the QHL but, for a brief time, he was on the other side of the puck. "When Val was first picked up by Remparts coach Ron Racette, I was playing for Trois Rivières Draveurs. Just days before Val had gotten to Quebec, there was a big brawl between our two teams and I had slapped around one of the Quebec players. Shortly after that game, Racette brought Val to Quebec. Before long, the news media and the fans were in a frenzy about this black American player from Long Island named Valmore James. The stories were being spread how this new guy had gotten into a fight in one of his first games with Quebec and his opponent tried to block a punch using his forearm. It was said that one punch from this Valmore James fellow broke the other guy's arm, causing a compound fracture."

As Pierre explains, in hockey, your opponent one day might be your roommate the next. "My Trois Rivières team soon had another game against Quebec. I skated over to Val and gave him a tap on the pads with my stick. We looked at each other and he had this fierce look in his eyes. We separated without anything happening but I will never forget that look. It was a look that could change people's minds. Just a couple days after that game, I was traded to the Remparts. I was much happier to be Val's teammate."

I hadn't set out to build a reputation as "just" a tough guy; I wanted to show that I was a hard-working player with my best hockey yet to come. Again, that's not to say that the fighting was separate and apart from the game. They were inseparable. If our opponents thought the best way to slow our most skilled players was to hack and cheap-shot them, they would also have to know that there was a price for that. In my eyes, an attack on one of us was an attack on us all. The clearer I delivered that message in each fight, the less I would need to do it in the future. A broken jaw here and a broken arm there delivered that message loud and clear. Suddenly, all of us had more room to skate. We could concentrate more on offense and defense and less on the likelihood that one of us would be two-hand-chopped from behind.

My rough and tumble style of play made me popular with our home fans. A hit song making the rounds back then was "Black Superman" by Johnny Wakelin. It was about Muhammad Ali, the heavyweight champ. The chorus celebrated, "Muhammad,

Muhammad Ali. He floats like a butterfly and stings like a bee. Muhammad, the black Superman." When I took to the ice in Quebec, our home-arena organist would play the chorus from "Black Superman." That always gave our fans an extra charge.

Another guy who created space for us was my friend Nelson Burton. Nelson was a maniac, and I mean that as a compliment. We would always try to outdo each other. Early in the game, I would run a player through the boards and Nelson would come on the ice and try to crush the next guy even worse. Then it would be my turn again. We would try to set a precedent in the first shifts of the game. We'd go out there and bang everything that moved. We wanted them to know that if they were going to touch the puck, there was a certain amount of physical contact that came with that. And if they were going to go into the corners, they weren't coming out.

That's not to say that the rough stuff was confined to our side alone. The two hardest hits I ever took in my career, which also resulted in the only two concussions I ever had, both came in the QHL. The first came on an open ice check from Rik Garcia of Hull Festivals early on during my first season. I didn't see him coming and he flat out crushed me. I never left my skates but I was out on my feet. I had tunnel vision. I tried to keep up with the play but I kept skating in the wrong direction. I crashed into Hull's goalie and he helped guide me back to the bench. I went to the locker room to clear my head and came back in the game when the cobwebs were gone.

The other particularly nasty shot I took came in a neutral site game at Sept-Îles. We were playing the Sorel Éperviers ("Black Hawks"). In that game, Lucien DeBlois hit me harder than I have ever been hit, on or off the ice. I was playing left wing and a teammate sent me a suicide pass that required me to take my eye off the approaching skater. I looked up a split second before DeBlois hit me, shoulder to chest. It was a full-on collision of Mack Trucks. He hit me so hard he cracked my sternum. As the wind was knocked out of me, a lung-full of blood flew from my mouth, covering Louie's jersey. We just stood there, staring at each other. DeBlois asked, "Are you OK, Val?" I could barely choke out my response, "I will be."

Our trainer brought me into the locker room. I coughed and a mass of clotted blood came out. The trainer was shocked, "Val, you're ruptured inside."

"I'm fine," I responded, and to prove it, I pointed out that each subsequent cough contained less blood. I was trying to talk my way back into the game but the trainer wasn't having it. I did return to play the following night. A week later, my chest felt itchy on the inside. I assumed it was from the healing taking place in there. My breathing was heavy for a few weeks too, so I tried to avoid the deep breaths that made me sound like a train going up the side of a mountain.

As bad as the hit from DeBlois was, it was still only the second worst experience of that trip for me. To get to Sept-Îles from Quebec City, we took a prop plane. I didn't like to fly under the best of circumstances. This wasn't the best of circumstances. The plane was a disaster. It was leaning sideways on the runway. When we got on board, the staff was joking that the plane had been a DC-9 but it was now a DC-6 because it had crashed three times. Yeah, real funny. I sat down in my seat but it was broken and it fell all the way back. Then there was a delay before we took off when they had to take some of the luggage off the plane because it was too heavy for the plane to get off the ground. It was a real bumpy flight and I was a mess. They tell me my hands went white from how tight I was gripping the hand rests, and my lips went pale from clenching my jaw. I can't tell you myself what colors I was turning because I refused to open my eyes the whole trip.

Sept-Îles was also the scene of another memorable Remparts game. There were no boards separating players on the bench from fans sitting behind them. This particular night, there was a drunk fan behind our bench, running his mouth the whole game. He was taunting us, cursing, spitting, and throwing beer on us. Finally, that fan, or maybe it was someone else, hit Coach Racette with a beer can. Nelson Burton and I needed no further invitation to jump into the stands, and our team followed. Any and every one in the area got mowed down. It didn't break up until there were no more people left to hit. The local police had to escort our team out of the arena.

A few days later, Nelson and I each received a summons charging us with assault. The drunk guy was claiming that we punched the shit out of him. We didn't hurt him too badly, but he did wind up with a broken nose and a bloody eye. The Remparts provided us with legal counsel. When we went before the judge, our young star defenseman, Kevin Lowe, a celebrated Quebec native who would go on to win multiple Stanley Cups with the Oilers dynasty of the '80s, testified to our good character. In Quebec, the hockey players were regarded almost as gods. The captains of the teams were highly respected, and the "C" or the "A" sewn on their sweater brought along an unofficial stamp of authority, even off the ice. Kevin's defense of us carried a lot of weight. The assault charges were dismissed and we were each ordered to pay a fine, a fine that the team quickly paid on our behalf.

Like Sept-Îles, the town of Sorel was an unfriendly place to play. Let's just say it was a town of limited etiquette. It was called blue collar but it was so rough and crass that you'd be better calling it a black collar town. It was in Sorel that I learned that in French, maybe the most beautiful language in the world, the word "nigger" is still "nigger." From the minute I got on the ice in Sorel, the racial insults were a constant.

Sorel was also a place where an army helmet might have done us more good than our hockey helmets. The arena had screen fencing that wrapped around the whole rink. The fans would throw change and flick lit cigarettes at us through the screen. During one game, a cigarette got down the sweater of one of my teammates. He was dancing around like James Brown and we had to strip him down on the bench to get the cigarette out. As always, I tried to make the best of a bad situation so, one night, I was able to collect better than two bucks in change that had been thrown at me. I stashed the coins in my hockey socks and silently thanked the Sorel Neanderthals for buying that night's first round.

TWELVE

THE RUDE TREATMENT WE RECEIVED in some smaller Quebec towns only made us appreciate beautiful Quebec City even more. The fans were very supportive of the team and the players. Of course, we worked hard at our game but we also enjoyed the benefits of playing in a city with a lot to offer its beloved hockey players.

Each of my years in Quebec, we were one of the biggest teams in the league. In fact, our Remparts junior squad was physically bigger than a number of the teams in the NHL. The first year I played in Quebec also happened to be Ron Racette's first year as coach. We made the playoffs and then reached the finals against the Sherbrooke Castors, the defending league champions. Sherbrooke finished the regular season with 51 wins and just 12 losses and nine ties. We had played Sherbrooke eight times during the regular season and managed only a single tie.

No one gave us much hope against Sherbrooke and their excellent goalie, Richard Sevigny. Being 18, I must have been too young and naive to see it the same way. I gave a television interview before the QHL Finals in which I claimed, in my best French, that Quebec City would win the series in six games. My teammates made sure I didn't have to eat those words. We won the series in six, and I netted a goal in the clincher. We were awarded the President's Cup as the champions of the QHL. Next up was the Memorial Cup round robin tournament to crown Canada's national junior champion.

As I mentioned before, our Remparts team was big — really big. Then we got to the Memorial Cup and saw one of our opponents, the New Westminster Bruins. These guys looked like professional football players on skates. As big as Barry Beck and Harold Phillipoff were, they didn't even stand out amongst the monsters on their team. Just looking at them, it was no wonder that they were the defending Memorial Cup champions.

Our captain was Jean Gagnon. He wasn't big, only about 5-foot-6, but he was one of the most talented players I ever saw. Early on in the first game against New Westminster, Jean had the puck and only had to get around Phillipoff for a clear shot at the net. Harold just smothered him. I had a good series and scored a couple goals, but the Bruins beat us in both games.

During the series, I was repeatedly baited with racial insults by a particularly mouthy lowlife on the New Westminster roster. Don Hobbins was one of the few Bruins players who didn't quite reach 6-foot-2. He kept skating past me, calling me a "nigger" among other slurs. He backed up his words every time by skating away and hiding behind bigger teammates. I was furious and I didn't care how big his buddies were. I skated over to the Bruins bench where the bomb thrower was sitting between Beck and Phillipoff. Not surprisingly, this hero refused to come back on the ice and back up his words. It took all my strength not to rip his chicken ass off the bench and slam him through the ice. I knew how important the tournament was and, in the back of my mind,

I knew that what I was planning to do to this prick would likely result in my suspension and my team having to play shorthanded for a long, long time.

I pointed my finger in his face, "You're a fucking punk. When I get the chance, I'm gonna tear your fucking head off." I then turned to Beck and Phillipoff. "I got no problem with you guys, you gotta know this motherfucker crossed the line, but I'm right here if you want some of this too." Barry and Harold looked away.

In the handshake line at the end of the game, Barry congratulated me on a good series and said that he expected he would see me again down the road.

Mr. Big Mouth also tried to shake my hand, "No hard feelings." I slapped his hand away. "Remember, you little fuck, I will see you again someday. Just remember that." It would take two more years but, like my guarantee in the QHL Finals, I would keep this promise too.

Remarkably, the Bruins went on to lose the Memorial Cup to the Hamilton Fincups, a team we had handled earlier in the tournament.

Although we didn't win the Canadian national junior championship, Quebec City was excited about our team. And we felt the same way about the city. Quebec City sits on the banks of the Saint Lawrence River and has a history dating back 500 years. Ancient stone buildings and stone walls line the cobblestone streets. Quebec City also has more than its fair share of pubs, clubs . . . and beautiful French-Canadian women. A wonderful combination for a young hockey player.

Each February, the city hosts the Quebec Winter Carnival. Picture Mardi Gras with snow and you'll get the idea. One evening during the festival, I slipped out after curfew, along with

Chris Brinster and a few of our other teammates. A favorite local watering hole was a place called My Uncle Charlie's. A manager at the bar invited us to visit a new place he had recently opened. We accepted the invitation and headed on over. After a minute or two of wrestling with the language barrier posed by the French-speaking doormen, we were let in as friends of the manager. We were brought to a private room where we spent some time sampling the beverages.

A bartender came back into the room and asked if I would help him carry cases of beer up from the basement. How could I refuse after the terrific hospitality we were being shown? Down in the basement, I leaned over to pick up several cases of beer when the bartender gave me an unexpected compliment. Specifically, he told me I had a great ass. Of course, I thanked him for noticing but then I told him that I wasn't interested. When we returned back upstairs, I noticed that the main bar area had filled with patrons, most of whom were men disco dancing with one another.

I went back to our private room and let my friends know that we were in a gay bar. Our concern about being caught in a bar after curfew quickly grew into concern that Coach Racette would catch us in a gay bar after curfew. I was catching enough shit for being black, but a hockey player who was black and gay . . .

My mates and I started our journey back to the rooming house, now thoroughly paranoid about being discovered by our coach. We were creeping through shadows and alleys, ducking from every passing car as Racette was known to do random checks of the bar area of town. One car drove slowly past and we leaned in behind some trash cans in front of another tavern. While we waited for the car to pass, there was a tapping on the bar window. I looked up to see a figure in the darkness waving his cock at me from behind a potted plant. "You gotta be fuckin' kidding me, what is up with tonight?"

The man behind the plant then moved closer to the window and I saw it was Curt Brackenbury, waving his dick at me and laughing his ass off. Curt was a friend and mentor to me from his days as an enforcer for the Long Island Cougars. While I was on the Remparts, Curt played for the Quebec Nordiques of the WHA. My friends and I went into the bar for a nightcap with Curt and his Nords teammate Serge Bernier.

Looking back, we did spend a good amount of time hiding from Coach Racette after curfew. One particularly close call came when three of us were at a table, trying to impress an equal number of lovely young ladies. We looked up and saw Ron come in the front door, scanning the crowd. The three of us squeezed underneath the table and Ron's feet came close enough for us to shine his shoes.

Ron wanted us home sleeping so we would be fresh for our games. Not that our hockey suffered. After coming close to the Memorial Cup during my first season in Quebec, our team was a heavy favorite the following year. In QHL play, we finished that next season in first place with 41 wins against 21 losses and 10 ties. In the league's playoff finals, it was Sherbrooke's turn to repay our upset of them the previous season, and they beat us to move on to the Memorial Cup. Just like that, my two years in Quebec City were finished. It was now time to consider where hockey might bring me next. My first hopes were pinned on the upcoming NHL draft.

THIRTEEN

ONE HUNDRED AND EIGHTY-FIVE names were called in the 1977 NHL amateur draft. The name "Valmore James" was called at number one hundred and eighty-four. Better late than never: I had been drafted by the Detroit Red Wings.

There was no ESPN back then, no internet, no live coverage of the draft. The day of the draft, I stayed at home with my family hoping for my phone to ring. When the day dragged on with no news, it seemed that I might not get that call. Then, finally, I heard from Buzz Deschamps and Sam Gregory, two former Long Island Ducks players who had been mentors to me and many other young hockey players on the Island. Buzz and Sam were plugged in with people in the NHL, so they got the first word of my selection by the Wings and passed the news on to me.

A few days after the draft, a letter from the team arrived at my house, congratulating me on my selection and providing details of the training camp I was to attend at the end of the summer. My dad and I must have read that letter 100 times. Seven years after I first laced up a pair of skates, I was a draft pick of the Detroit Red Wings, an American team and one of the NHL's Original Six. My mind filled with daydreams of the huge impression I was going to make in camp. Hell, I could even see myself giving the team no other choice than to put me on the opening day roster. Of course, I knew the odds of that happening were less than slim, but I was determined to aim high.

I worked hard that summer, skating almost every day and following the exercise schedule sent to me by the team. I kissed my folks goodbye and hopped in my car, heading out to the Wings camp in Kalamazoo, Michigan. When I arrived, my fantasies collided hard with reality. There were hundreds of players there. As Buzz and Sam had warned me, almost all the spots on the roster of the big club were already spoken for. Just about every one of the rest of us was being evaluated to see if we were worthy of one of the also-limited spots in the team's minor league system. The numbers were against me but I still had an opportunity to be noticed, an opportunity for a professional contract. I felt I was ready.

After our physical exams, we jumped right into camp. The training regimen was intense. There were morning ice sessions on hockey fundamentals followed by afternoon scrimmages. Before and after the ice sessions were exhausting exercise programs including many hours of running and weight lifting.

The first morning I was at camp, I was surprised to see someone familiar through the crowd of skaters. Amongst the hundreds of players attending this camp was the punk from New Westminster who had called me every imaginable racial slur two seasons earlier during the Memorial Cup. Hobbins. I had forgotten neither the name nor the face. Unfortunately for him, I hadn't forgotten his words either. I promised him back then that our paths would cross again and I would pay him back. Hockey is funny that way. You never know when and where you will run into a former teammate or opponent.

During the Memorial Cup, this guy was able to hide behind his bigger teammates. Now, at the Red Wings camp, he was amongst mostly strangers, each of whom was much more interested in their own showing than in sticking up for someone they didn't know and who was competing for the same job they wanted. As soon as I set my eyes on him, my original fury bubbled back to the surface. I found it hard to focus on anything but this punk and the disgusting and disrespectful way that he had treated me. There was no doubt that this camp was going to be the place that he was going to answer for his insults. The only question was when it would happen. I wouldn't have to wait for long.

On the second afternoon of camp, I found myself opposite this character during the intra-squad scrimmage. I ran hard into him and he just stared at me. "You got something to say now, you fuckin' punk?" He continued to stand there, frozen, so I cross-checked him. "Nowhere to hide now, tough guy." I cross-checked him again and we both dropped our gloves. I went orangutan on him, punching him straight down to the ice.

The echo of his racist slurs filled my head and I completely lost it. I kept beating on him. In the back of my mind, I could hear whistles blowing and voices yelling to stop. I didn't let up. I couldn't. He had hurt me deeper than I realized and now all I wanted to do was make him feel some hurt too. I continued to hammer away on him when my skates got kicked out from underneath me and I fell heavily to the ice. A skate glided past my hand, nearly severing my fingers. I jumped up, still furious, and growled, "Who's the fuckin' asshole who kicked my skates out?" Unfortunately for me, the answer to my question was "Coach Bobby Kromm." He looked at me and said, "Get off the ice."

My scrimmage day was done. The following day I was cut

from the Wings camp and sent to the adjacent Kalamazoo Wings minor league camp. A few days later, I was cut altogether. In my exit interview, the team told me I needed to work on my skating and puck handling. But I hadn't been drafted for my puck handling ability. I knew that there was another reason that I was let go. The teams want players who are physical and on the edge, ready to commit violence at the drop of a hat. But they don't like it if they can't control you. I had lost all control. As a result, I lost my first, best shot at a pro contract.

After being cut by Detroit, I called my dad. He was working the phones with my other hockey guardian angels, guys like Buzz, Sam, John Muckler, and Norm Ryder, who many times over the years helped me find a hockey home. This time, they got me a shot in nearby Sioux City with the Musketeers of the United States Hockey League. Sioux City was a senior league team. The senior leagues were, in many ways, a last chance league for those looking to play pro hockey. If you didn't get a pro contract after juniors, it was much more difficult to get noticed in the seniors. This was a place for former pros who were looking to skate a while longer before hanging them up or, like me, players who were still hoping for another chance. The caliber of hockey was high but, for many, playing senior hockey was the last stop.

I played several months in Sioux City, making friends with teammates like Bob Beatty and Jim Peck. We were paid almost nothing. I supplemented my meager paycheck by landscaping. When the short season ended in Sioux City, my dad and his friends found some more senior league spots for me in Mississauga, Ontario. My next obstacle would be getting to Canada.

My drive from Sioux City to Mississauga happened to take place during the Great Blizzard of 1978, which dumped two feet of snow all along my route. When the roads became too treacherous, I pulled into a truck stop to wait out the weather. I was happy to be off the road and eating a warm meal. I was also enjoying the company of a friendly waitress. She was cute but a bit on the thick side. Still, as they say, any port in a storm. And this was a storm for the ages.

My new friend invited me to rest my bones on a cot she kept in a backroom. As soon as the words left her mouth, time came to a standstill. Like a scene out of a movie, the jukebox went silent, the clock stopped ticking, and I became very aware of the eyes of a dozen unfriendly truck drivers turned my way. I could see how this movie might end for the black protagonist, so I politely declined the gal's offer and slowly slipped back out to the parking lot.

Continuing my drive towards Canada, I wondered whether this would be the last time I was traveling to a hockey job. If this was the end of the line for my playing career, why shouldn't I just turn my car around now and head back home to Long Island? As always, my dad had again encouraged me not to give in to the doubts. Still, the doubts were making some good points. I was only 20 years old, but I had no professional contract. I had been given a look and I was let go. Now, I was heading, in a blizzard, back to Canada to play more senior division hockey, a place rarely scouted by the pro teams. Frankly, it wasn't looking good.

As I drove along the frozen highway towards Mississauga, alone except for my doubts, I saw loose paper blowing in the road ahead of me. From a distance, it looked like confetti. As I got closer, I could make out green confetti. Closer still, I saw that it was cash, blowing around the highway. I stopped and gathered up several hundred dollars in five-, ten-, and twenty-dollar bills. I wasn't looking for a sign but finding this money in the street told me that I should stay on course and continue my trip to Canada. So there would be a couple more months of hockey, playing for the Golden Arrows and the Bee Hives of Mississauga. The decision of where to go from there wasn't going away, but it could wait until the end of the hockey season.

FOURTEEN

THE SUMMER I SPENT on Long Island following my "lost year" of senior league play convinced me to give my dream of playing pro hockey one last shot. If I wanted to make it to the American Hockey League, to within spitting distance of the NHL, I was going to have to first make a name for myself in the lower minor leagues. This would mean low pay and long bus trips, with even longer odds that anyone in the pro ranks would ever notice me.

I knew what I would be up against, but my dad and I had many heart-to-hearts that summer. He said I could walk away now with my head held high. First strapping on skates as a 13-year-old American kid, I had more than held my own in Canada, in both Junior A and Junior B hockey. I helped my team claim the Quebec Hockey League championship and we came within two wins of the Memorial Cup. Then I was an NHL draft pick. No one could ever take these things away from me.

I had already succeeded in hockey beyond anyone's imagination. I had exceeded everyone else's expectations but, as my dad put it, what about *my* expectations? When I closed my eyes as a kid, was it my dream to give up after junior hockey? Did I see myself stopping at this point? Of course not. My dream ended with me pulling on an NHL sweater.

My dad made me ask myself if that was still my dream and, if so, how badly did I want to achieve it? When I considered that my dad was a man who traveled a thousand miles with his young family to chase his own humble dream of a better life, it made my decision much easier. The next stop for me would be the City of Erie in northwestern Pennsylvania.

Once again, my dad's Long Island hockey cabal used its connections to find a spot for me in a pre-season camp. Ben Kasper, my dad's boss and the owner of the Long Island Cougars, had moved the team to Erie and the North Eastern Hockey League. The team was re-christened as the Erie Blades. The coach and general manager of the Blades was smart, tough hockey-lifer Nick Polano. Kasper recommended me to Polano, who agreed to give me a look. As always, the only guarantee that came with the invitation to camp was that I would have an opportunity to compete for a job. I paid my own way to Erie and only if I made the team would I be paid for my time there. Otherwise, I would be given only bus fare to return back home. I didn't think that would be a problem. My batteries were recharged and I was eager to prove myself.

At the same time I was packing to travel to Erie, I was contacted by Muzz MacPherson, the former Sault Ste. Marie coach who initially shot down my plan to play for Ron Racette in Quebec. He was also the guy who told me I made his team, only to cut me the following morning. Although I remembered him very well, it was obvious that he didn't remember me. Muzz was now coaching one of Erie's NEHL rivals, the Jersey Aces, and he invited me to his camp. I told him, "Sure, coach, I'll see you in

New Jersey in a couple of days." Then I jumped in my car and drove straight to Erie.

When I arrived for camp, I was put up at the local Howard Johnson motel. I was housed in a small room that was shared by six hockey players. The room was wall-to-wall bed, with cots crammed into every inch of the place. The one bathroom that was shared by the six of us was a place not fit for man nor beast.

The competition in camp was stiff. The Southern Hockey League had just folded and there were a lot of experienced hockey players looking for jobs. When the SHL folded, the Quebec Nordiques of the World Hockey Association lost their farm team in Tidewater, Virginia. The Blades then signed on as the Nordiques' new farm team so we had even more talented players making the trek between Erie and the big club in Quebec City. This pipeline with the Nords gave the Blades access to more than a few excellent French-Canadian players over the years, including Pierre Aubry, Pierre Lagace, and Sylvain Côté. There was no lack of talent or competition in our training camp.

In my first game with Erie, we went to Cherry Hill, New Jersey, to play the Aces in a pre-season exhibition. My dad drove up from Long Island with my brother Bobby to catch the game. Before I arrived in Erie, the Blades had gotten their asses kicked when they played a couple of earlier pre-season games. In our pregame warm-up in the Cherry Hill Arena, I skated passed the Aces bench. "Hello Muzz," I said, "it's good to see you." The coach looked at me, trying to place where he knew me from.

The game started and I was quiet at the beginning, sizing up our opposition. I scored an early goal and had returned to the bench when things got interesting. Brian Gustafson of the Aces speared my teammate Paul Skjodt. Paul was a skilled but somewhat inconsistent player. One day he might be the best skater on the ice and the next day he might skate straight into the boards. On this night, Gustafson snuck up behind Paul and drove the butt end of his stick into his gut. Paul fell to the ice and our trainer, Mike Caron, went out to help him.

I was on the bench and I looked over at Nick Polano. Nick didn't say a word, we just made eye contact and I knew immediately that we were thinking the same thing.

While the refs were tending to Paul, I quietly slipped off the bench and skated over like I had been on the ice the whole time. I stopped in front of Gustafson and I quickly learned that he wasn't as tough face-to-face as he thought he was when he was spearing guys from behind.

I gave him the beating he deserved. I was holding him up with one hand while I pounded him with the other.

One after another, three of his teammates stepped in to restore their team's pride and, one after another, I punched them to the ice. One of the contenders was this Peter Jack fellow who was said to be the toughest guy on the Aces. I gave him a one-sided beating too. The third guy to take his shot actually did a decent job and cut me over the eye. Unfortunately for him, seeing my own blood only took my anger to the next level. I let loose on this guy, opening him up from ear to ear.

As our trainer Mike recalls, "Val tore into this guy. When he was done, this kid's face looked like raw hamburger. I never saw that guy again and I think that he left hockey after that beating."

When I ran out of Aces to beat on, the refs decided it was a good time for me to hit the showers. Before leaving the ice, I again skated by the Aces bench. "Hey, Muzz, do you remember me now?"

I'm guessing that I got Muzz's attention that night but, more importantly, I got the attention of our own coach. After the game, Coach Polano told Robin Roberts Jr., the team's color commentator, "Oh, we're going to find a spot for Val on this team." With my dad watching from the stands, I had found my new hockey home.

Back then, Erie was the third largest city in Pennsylvania. The people were proud and hard working. For a long time, the area had been a thriving manufacturing center with plenty of good paying jobs in the plants operated by General Electric and Hammermill Paper, amongst many others. Unfortunately, many of these jobs were gone by 1978. And many more jobs were to leave soon after that. The city was looking for something to rally around but, until Nick Polano took over, the Blades didn't give them much of a reason to cheer. That was about to change.

FIFTEEN

WHEN I ARRIVED IN ERIE for the 1978–79 season, the team was just restarting operations after being dormant for a year. Ben Kasper had brought the team to Erie from Long Island, but his imported hockey management team had failed to connect with the local fans. A local Erie physician, John Caruso, had taken a small stake in the team ownership as payment for his services as the team doctor. Dr. Caruso believed that the success of the franchise depended on a much closer relationship between the team and the people of Erie.

As the good doctor himself explains, "One quiet evening while I was working in the hospital emergency room [during the 1976–77 playoffs], I called Ben Kasper and worked out a deal to buy the team. The sale was reported the next day in the local press." As Dr. Caruso predicted, the town was fired up about the local takeover of the Blades. The team had drawn a total of only 2,400 fans combined to the two playoff games that happened right before the sale was made public. The game following the announcement was packed with 3,600 fans.

Dr. Caruso replaced the general manager with Nick Polano, who was also named head coach and boss of all things hockey.

Nick was not from Erie, but it didn't hurt that he wore his Italian heritage on his sleeve in a town with a large population of Italian-Americans. Most importantly, Nick was about to become the town's biggest booster and cheerleader.

After the one season in which the league went dark, the 1978–79 season was the kickoff for the resurrected Eastern Hockey League. I had grown up with and around the Long Island Ducks of the old EHL so this was a homecoming of sorts to me.

Dr. Caruso gave the reins and full control of the team to Nick. He made all the team's hockey decisions as our coach and hockey commander. He did rely on a number of informal assistant coaches. The team's play-by-play broadcaster was JP Dellacamera. Today, JP is America's premiere soccer announcer. Back then, he ran public relations for Nick and the team. JP and I started in Erie at the same time but I already knew JP from his time on Long Island as the PR director of the Cougars. After his time on the Island, JP had gone to Hampton, Virginia, with John Brophy when Brophy was hired to coach the Gulls in the Southern Hockey League. JP had been a friend to both me and my dad, so I was glad to see that he was part of what we were trying to build in Erie. Robin Roberts Jr. handled the color commentary as JP's on-air partner. Mike Caron was our trainer and Ron Sciarrilli ran much of the team's business operations. In addition to their assigned duties, each of these guys was also an assistant and trusted advisor to Nick.

Nick himself was a good fit for me from the start. He had also come from humble roots — Sudbury, Ontario — where his options were either to succeed in hockey or to work in the local mines. As Robin said, "Nick got a 20-game contract with the old St. Louis Braves where Phil Esposito was his teammate. Nick had

15 fights in the 20 games and stayed for good." That was a career path I could relate to. I was also encouraged by the fact that my old friend Nicky Fotiu had tremendous success playing for Nick Polano. As the player-coach of the Cape Cod Cubs of the North American Hockey League, Polano had coached Fotiu's first year of hockey outside of the New York Met League. From there, Nicky went on to a 17-year pro career.

All of the signs looked good at the beginning and Nick did not disappoint. He knew exactly what he wanted to do with each piece that he added to our team. With an eye for both talent and chemistry, he had keen instinct for how a guy played and how that player would fill a need on the team. He also made decisions based on what a player was like in the locker room and how he interacted with his teammates. Nick had a knack for finding unappreciated talent on struggling teams and bringing them to Erie where they excelled. I respected how he sought input from his guys about other players he was considering bringing to Erie. He valued our opinions about what a new guy could bring to the team.

Nick built the team around men like Stan Gulutzan, Steve Stockman, and Brad Rhiness, who would score 100 goals between them that year. Nick also signed the high-scoring Paul Mancini, who had been Wayne Gretzky's linemate in Sault Ste. Marie and was later a first-round draft pick of the Los Angeles Kings. Danny Poulin was our rookie of the year defenseman. Our primary goalie was Carey Walker, the Memorial Cup champion from the New Westminster Bruins who was also the older brother of future baseball Hall of Famer, Larry Walker. Besides bringing in these stars who could have excelled on other levels, Nick built a deep roster of players who had skill, size, and character. This included Paul Devlin, Ron Hansis, Pierre Lagace, Paul Pacific, and Paul Sheard, amongst many others who could play and didn't mind getting dirty while doing so.

We rolled through the regular season, finishing in first place with a record of 47 wins, 19 loses, and 3 ties. We were good and we weren't shy about it. We could score, we could defend, we could check, and we could throw fists. The hard-working people of Erie responded to the similar hard work that they saw us put into every game. Something special was building between the players and their adopted home.

Nick was big on the players getting engaged with the Erie community. Not only were we encouraged to accept speaking engagements and attend social events with the fans, we were often invited into their homes to have dinner and meet their families. That first year was the beginning of the love affair between the town of Erie and its players. And the feeling was mutual. Some of the guys never left Erie. To this day, Sylvain Côté, Paul Mancini, and Pierre Lagace live in the area.

After dominating the regular season, we were extremely confident going into the post season. In the first round of the playoffs, we beat the Utica Mohawks, four games to one. Then we played the Hampton Aces for the Mitchell Cup in the league finals. Halfway through the regular season, the Aces and their coach, Muzz MacPherson, had relocated the team from New Jersey to Hampton, Virginia.

To our surprise, we went down 3 games to 1 in the finals. After the season we had, anything less than winning the championship would be an enormous choke. We won Game 5 at home but we still needed to win Game 6 in Hampton. Coach Polano came in the locker room and poured a bag of $100 bills on the floor. "You win tonight, boys, and this is yours to spend however you like." We won Game 6 and then spent the night partying before flying back to Erie.

We arrived in Erie in the middle of the night and there were 4,000 people waiting for us at the airport. It was incredible. They led us back to the arena in a parade, a long caravan of cars.

The next day was Game 7, and the traffic to the arena was backed up for miles. We needed the police to escort our bus to the building. It was still cold in Western Pennsylvania but the crowd in the Erie County Field House was thousands over capacity and the heat in the building caused a fog to build up on the ice. We had to skate around in circles to clear the fog. In the third period, I scored a goal and we held on the rest of the way with Hampton controlling the puck in our end, making my goal the series clincher.

The town went nuts. We celebrated all night, first closing all the bars and then all the after-hours joints. The next night, we had a team party at the Holiday Inn. Some of the players got a bit rambunctious and took the instruments from the band and tried to play. A nervous manager called the police but the cops knew all of us. This was our town.

A parade was held in downtown Erie with the players riding in new Jeeps that were loaned to us by a local auto dealership that was also a team sponsor. There were thousands and thousands of people cheering us on. At the end of the parade route, a number of the guys drove off with the Jeeps and went four-wheeling. One of the Jeeps was found on the peninsula that jutted out into Lake Erie.

The next two seasons were no less successful. It was said that our Blades team was built like a minor league version of the Broad Street Bullies. We had size, we were physical, we had guys who could put the puck in the net, we had strong goaltending.

Nick kept the core of our team together and I had many of the same teammates for all three years that I played in Erie. Nick also brought in a couple new pieces each year, adding beasts like Syl Côté and Nelson Burton to what was already the most physically dominant team in the league. We played on the opposite side of Pennsylvania than the Flyers but I don't think it was any coincidence that our jerseys were the same orange and black colors as were worn by the Bullies.

Our opponents and their fans hated us because we were good — and because we knew we were good. Of course, you always want to be humble, but sometimes it wasn't easy. One night, after we beat Utica 14–1 in the opening game of a playoff series, I was hounded for a quote by the Utica beat reporter. I figured he was looking for some verbal slight that the home team might post in their locker room for inspiration. I told him, "C'mon, no one can tell how the series is going to go after one game." But I didn't want to lie, so I continued, "Let's wait at least two games." In the second game, we thumped them again, getting us halfway to what would be a four-game sweep.

There's no doubt that when I came to Erie, my skills were unpolished. I felt that Nick brought out the best in my game. With hard work, and under Nick's tutelage, I became a much better hockey player. I had been brought in for my size and, let's face it, my fighting ability, but Nick gave me more and more responsibilities in critical situations, and as my skating improved and my confidence increased, I became a better player. Nick liked my shot from the left point so he encouraged me to take it when it was open. He also started using me on the power play, putting me down low as a big body in front of the net. I wasn't easy to move out from the top of the crease and I created traffic in front of the goalie, similar to the power forwards that came to dominate in the 1990s NHL. Nick helped me with my discipline so, while he never discouraged me from kicking some ass, I was careful not to take penalties that put the team in a bad spot.

Each of my three years in Erie ended with us winning the Mitchell Cup. During this time, Nick Polano was also named the minor league hockey executive of the year by the *Hockey News*. If all our on-ice success wasn't special enough, we even had the opportunity to play the greatest team in the world, the Soviet national team.

The Erie Blades hosted the Soviets one week before the 1980 Olympics in Lake Placid. The Field House was jam-packed and all of our fans were waving American flags. As much as I would like to take credit, I can't say that we softened up the Soviets for the American Miracle. But it is possible that the Russians were tired from skating circles around us. Because of call-ups and injuries, we did not present them with the best team we had in Erie. I doubt it would have mattered. We played well for the first six minutes or so, but after we hit a goalpost, the Soviets put on a show. It was just an incredible display of hockey skill.

Sylvain was built like a big Quebec farmer, a seriously strong man. He threw a bodycheck on one of the Soviet players and bounced right off him. I was on defense that night and I tried to take the puck away from the legendary Valeri Kharlamov. He was half my size, so how hard could it be? Well, Kharlamov left me with a souvenir that I still have to this day, a pinky finger that points in the wrong direction. He spun around me with the puck velcroed to his stick blade. I reached out to grab him but he flew right past me, twisting my pinky out of the socket.

That Soviet team was something to see. Not only were we

playing the best team in the world but maybe the best in history. And they were absolute gentlemen. They beat us 9–0 but they could have scored 20 goals. That was a special night during a special time in Erie, not just for the town's hockey fans but also for those of us who were fortunate enough to play there.

SIXTEEN

MY FIRST CONTRACT WITH the Erie Blades paid me 200 bucks a week. Even in 1978, that was chicken scratch, especially when you consider that we were only paid for the six or seven months of the hockey season. Our coach, Nick, was not only a smart hockey man but a shrewd businessman too. He would bring in players who had no wives or families to support, so we wouldn't be as dependent on the money. Nick would also have all the players eat together at team meals. This helped build team camaraderie. And it didn't hurt Nick's feelings that these team meals were cheaper than giving us meal money.

We were always looking for ways to stretch our meager paychecks. Every little bit helped.

One of our guys, Paul Mancini, came to Erie shortly before Christmas and his contract had a bunch of performance bonuses for scoring a certain number of goals. When he would get close to a performance bonus, Nick would sit him on the bench. Then, if we needed a goal and Nick had no choice, he would put Manny back on the ice. We would do the dirty work to get Manny the puck and he would bury it. When he scored one of his "money goals," he would do a lap around the ice and then slide on his knees towards the goal, pointing his stick at the goalie like it was a machine gun. We all celebrated too because Manny was a generous guy and he always shared the party when he got one of those bonuses.

To save a few bucks, most of the players also shared living quarters. The first place I stayed was known as the "United Nations House." My housemates were our trainer Mike Caron, an American from Maine who was fluent in French; my former Remparts teammate Pierre Lagace, a French-Canadian; and Floyd Lahace, a Native-American player from Quebec whose last name meant "the axe" in French, an accurate description for how he wielded his stick on the ice. And then there was me, maybe the rarest of all the nationalities in the UN House, a black hockey player from New York.

Living together and working together and playing together left few secrets between the members of our team. Those tight living arrangements sometimes resulted in the sharing of, as they say today, way too much information. Some of which, of course, I will now share.

One of the guys in our house had a serious girlfriend. She was older than us, which wasn't saying much as we were barely into our twenties. It was still the 1970s and this gal was a sweet, pretty hippie chick. We used to tease our friend, "Hey, it's nice to see you're dating your grandmother." But when his girlfriend spent the night, no one could sleep. Her screams of ecstasy shrieked through the house for hours. The next morning, she would come downstairs and join us for breakfast, acting like nothing happened. Inevitably, one of our overtired group at the kitchen table would pass a remark on her house-shaking performance, "Should I pass the sausage or did you have enough of that last night?" She took it all in the good fun that it was intended.

Another one of our one-time housemates was known to love his beer. The problems arose when he drank too much of that beer. When it came time to relieve his bladder, he would urinate wherever he happened to be at that moment. Many times, we would have to pull this guy out of the corners of bars and restaurants and steer him to the bathroom or outside to the parking lot. On one road trip, I was awakened in the middle of the night when my friend let himself into our motel room. He was sleepwalking. They say you should never wake a sleepwalker. Unless, that is, he is trying to take a leak on you. My friend stopped at the foot of the bed and started pissing on my bed before I woke him up and chased him, his cock in his hand, out of the room.

Of course, I was the subject of some UN House stories myself but, since this is my book, I get to pick which ones are told here. Then again, I'm too humble to tell the next story. But not so humble that I would stop my old friend, Mike Caron, from telling it.

"Val was scared of the dark . . ."

OK, Mike might be exaggerating about that part.

"Val was scared of the dark. Even on the bus, he kept the dome light on. At home, he would sleep with the lights on and a blanket pulled over his head. He also slept in the nude. He had the most incredible physique, completely chiseled. It was ridiculous because he didn't really exercise and his diet consisted of Burger King and Coca-Cola. If that wasn't unfair enough, he was also ridiculously endowed. When we had women visitors, Val could inspire them to find religion. We would tell them to peek in Val's room where he was sleeping. They would open the door and see Val snoring away, with the lights on and the blanket pulled over his head. His naked lower half would be exposed. The women would all gasp, 'Oh, my God!'"

More tales were born during the times we spent outside of our house. From the beginning, Nick had encouraged us to get involved in the community. In Erie, the regulars on the team went out to certain taverns on certain nights of the week. While helping to further build our team spirit, these mixers also allowed the players to mingle with fans from the community. More than that, when we started winning, the good people of Erie made it a little easier on our wallets. The town loved its hockey team and we were treated like local celebrities. There were more than a dozen bars and restaurants where our money was no good, which was a good thing, considering what Nick was paying us.

One of the places we would go after a game was the Penalty Box Club at the Erie Ramada Inn. One night, I was there with Sylvain. Syl was an excellent hockey player, when he managed to stay on the ice. He would spend about 350 minutes each season cooling his heels in the penalty box. That is the equivalent of six full games spent watching from the bin. But even with his many time-outs, Syl was still good for at least 30 goals a year. While he was much more than a policeman on the ice, he later became one off the ice, eventually trading in his hockey stick for a badge as one of Northeast PD's finest. But I'm not sure you would have bet on either of us going into law enforcement this particular night at the Penalty Box Club.

Syl had his eyes on a local girl who he had been scoping out for a couple weeks. While at the bar, I pointed out to Syl that the object of his affection was disco dancing with someone else. Her partner was dressed head to toe like Travolta in *Saturday Night Fever*, except his head didn't match his threads. He just looked too nerdy for the part. With his coke-bottle glasses, he was more like an accountant than a Casanova. But, there was no denying, this geek was a terrific dancer. Unfortunately for him, it was also painfully obvious that he was wearing a cheap toupee.

I needled my buddy Syl a bit, "With moves like that, you know he's gonna take her home tonight."

Syl complained, "You gotta be kidding me. She's dancing with that loser? Fuck that."

I chuckled, "What can you do, Syl? He's just got better moves than you. And better hair." I went back to my drink.

A moment later, I looked up to notice that Syl's seat at the bar was empty. Looking through the crowd, I saw Syl, in his suit, crawling through the customers towards the dance floor. As the geek danced close by, Syl jumped up and snatched the toupee off his head and tossed it across the room. The guy stopped doing the hustle and chased his flying squirrel hat across the dance floor.

The following week, Syl and I had stopped at another local club for a nightcap when we saw the same odd couple. By this point, Syl had lost interest in the gal, but not in the sport of tweaking the geek. On this evening, the dancing fool apparently had too much to drink and was nodding off at a table with his date. Syl strolled by and again snatched the guy's toupee, launching it across the room. Well, as they say, it's all fun and games until someone files a complaint with the police. Which this guy did.

All ended well for Syl as he was able to turn this potential legal mess into a positive, life-changing experience. To answer Baldy's complaint, Syl had to hire a French-speaking lawyer, and there was only one in Erie. It was at this lawyer's office that Syl met the lawyer's pretty receptionist, Debra. She and Syl have been married now for more than 25 years.

Syl wasn't the only one to come to Erie to play hockey, only to settle down there with a local gal. At one point, my friend and housemate Pierre Lagace was called up to the Nordiques of the WHA. After a time, he came back to the Blades. When Pete returned to Erie, I picked him up from the airport and took him to breakfast at a local restaurant. While we were eating, Pete took notice of a pretty young woman working as the hostess. He asked me if I knew her. I told him I did, asking if he wanted me to make an introduction.

Pete got real serious and said, "Of course, I have to meet her, Val, because that is the woman I am going to marry." I thought that Pete was just being dramatic. My French-Canadian brothers could be that way in matters of romance. But I made the introduction and Pete did indeed marry that young lady. Pete and his wife, Pam, run the same restaurant to this day.

Not all of our social events had happy endings. One night, the team got together for a party at a club called Stack's Place in Northeast, a town a short distance from Erie. The club was the capper of a day spent touring local wineries. There are some terrific wineries in the Erie area and a day of wine-tasting was arranged as one of our many meet-and-greet events with the fans.

Later, at Stack's, some more beverages were tasted. During the evening festivities, one of our toughest players, Nelson Burton, got annoyed when he felt that our starting goaltender Carey Walker was making a pass at Burton's gal. He told Carey to knock it off, which only made Carey flirt even more. Nelson dragged Carey into the bathroom and threw him through the bathroom stalls, knocking them off the wall. The rest of us pulled Nelson out of the bathroom and he stomped out of the club. However, when he got to the parking lot, Nelson found that his car had four flat tires. He came back inside to find another one of our teammates, Truck Tebutt, laughing his ass off at

Nelson's sabotaged vehicle. Truck was a terrific defenseman, and a decent guy, but he had the gift — or curse — of pissing people off. Nelson punched Truck in the mouth and broke his jaw.

Our coach, Nick, was out of town that night with Dr. Caruso on team business. They returned to Erie to find that Carey's leg was in a splint, Truck's jaw was wired shut, and Stack's Place was trashed. Carey wound up missing our game against the Soviet team.

We were a helluva team, almost unbeatable on the ice, but we managed to do a number on ourselves that night at Stack's. To make sure that there was no similar nonsense for the rest of the season, Nick arranged to have a bus waiting for the team outside the arena after every game. As soon as the game ended, we were driven to a hotel in the sticks where we couldn't get into too much trouble.

As for the Stack's mess, by the next home game, vendors were selling T-shirts and bumper stickers that proclaimed, "I Survived the Erie Blades Northeast Tour at Stack's." At least someone was making a decent buck.

SEVENTEEN

WHILE SOME OF THE GUYS found lifelong love in Erie, others found more temporary company. As was the case in every level of hockey I ever played, there were a number of female fans in Erie who befriended the young men playing the game. Some might call these gals groupies, but I thought of them more as friends of the team. *Good* friends of the team.

It was while I was growing up on Long Island that I first came across a dedicated group of gals who enjoyed partying with the Ducks players after the games. One night, a particular Ducks player was out with one of these young ladies when things got heated inside the player's car. Apparently, the pair couldn't wait to get a room before starting their romantic activities. In fact, they didn't even wait until the car was parked. Understandably, the player got distracted. His car swerved off the road and plowed through a fence. Fortunately, no one was hurt, but a police officer came upon the accident almost immediately after it had happened.

The officer approached the player's car and asked him what had happened. The player replied, "You see, Officer, we were driving down the road and a dog ran out in front of us. I had to swerve to avoid running it over and we hit the fence."

The officer responded, "I understand that, Sir, but what happened to your clothes?" Both the player and his friend were completely naked.

"Well, you see, our clothes must have been knocked off by the force of the accident," he offered. Yeah, that's the ticket.

I have my own confessions of an encounter or two with some of these morale boosters. On one particular evening, I broke off from a postgame party and accompanied a friend of the team to her hotel room. This gal was cute enough, but we couldn't break free from her sister. To be more specific, we couldn't break free from her seriously homely sister. My date didn't seem to mind that her sister was watching us from a seat across the room, so who was I to complain?

After a couple minutes of fumbling around in the dark, I had almost forgotten that the Ugly Duckling was still in the room. But I soon became distracted from the task at hand by a strange noise coming from the shadows. At first, I couldn't place the sound. It sounded like slapping. As my eyes adjusted, I could make out a silhouette of the sister. She was pumping her fist up and down over her crotch, in time to the slapping sounds.

I whispered, "Sweetheart, I think your sister is jacking off." My date's "sister" turned out to be her cross-dressing, masturbating brother. Needless to say, that was enough to break the mood.

Another evening of "Three's Company" came about in Quebec City when a teammate and I were invited to the apartment of a French-Canadian dame we had just met in a local pub. She was probably equal in years to me and my buddy combined, but two-times-twenty only made her "mature" rather than "old." This lady had curves enough for two. And it's a good thing she did. Before you could say rub-a-dub-dub, she led us straight to

97

the bathroom and into her four-leg, cast-iron bathtub. Between the three of us, there was barely room for any water. It got so crowded during the pile-up, I couldn't be sure of whose body parts I was grabbing ahold of. Of course, that didn't stop us.

Young hockey players are no different than other boys and young men. Dating and carousing is part of growing up. For us, it was a time of learning about ourselves and the ways of the world. Our interest in the fairer sex was probably exceeded only by our interest in playing hockey.

Starting with my move to Canada during high school, every year or two, I was introduced to a new town and its young ladies. And the introduction was not always limited to younger gals.

As with all junior hockey players invited to live in local homes, I became an instant addition to whatever family happened to be my sponsor at the time. It was as if the stork had taken the long way when delivering me to them. I became their new, 6-foot, 180-pound bundle of joy.

Despite my size, I was still a teenager, a kid. And like all growing adolescents, I still needed feeding and care and nurturing. The mom and dad of the house became my surrogate parents. Their kids became my brothers and sisters. Since we were typically close in age, it was inevitable that, on occasion, the daughter of one house or another might become more of a "kissing cousin," rather than a "sister," to a hockey player living under the same roof. Hormone-fueled teenagers in close quarters might be expected to find each other's company. What I did not see coming was the slightly more mature company I found in one of my sponsor homes. Or perhaps it found me.

It began in the family room in front of the television. I was half asleep on the couch, sitting next to the mom of the house.

What started as an innocent rubbing of feet escalated into the seduction of a teenage boy by a beautiful woman twice his age. Believe me, I wasn't complaining. In what was the first extended relationship of my life, we had an affair that carried on for months. I felt guilty for betraying the trust of my sponsor family but, at that age, I was dealing with some powerful, new emotions. I just wasn't thinking with my head.

Unlike teenage couples who couldn't care less who knows about their relationships, I had to be very careful that no one would find out about us. We both did. I was paranoid that something I said or did would give us away. With our difference in age and race, I could only imagine the scandal that would have erupted if word ever got out. I'm sure it would have been the end of her family. Would it also have been the end of my hockey career? Fortunately, we never had to find out the answer to these questions. We were able to keep our secret intact and we went back to our separate worlds when I returned to New York at the end of the season.

EIGHTEEN

A TEAM'S ABILITY TO SUCCEED on the road separated the
men from the boys in the Eastern Hockey League. Our team was
all but untouchable at home in Erie. At one point, we won 26
straight games at the Field House. Our success ratcheted up the
level of hostility we faced in the opposing arenas. Nothing could
send the other team's fans home happier than beating the Erie
Blades. Nothing except, of course, wounding and maiming the
Blades along the way. We always knew that there was nothing
less than outright hatred waiting for us at the end of every long
bus trip to an away game. Going into these road arenas was not
for the faint of heart. I thrived on it.

Our closest neighbor in the EHL was the Johnstown Wings,
just under 200 miles south of Erie. Despite this geographical
closeness, there was never any doubt going into Johnstown that
we were entering hostile enemy territory. Johnstown was the
inspirational home of the Charlestown Chiefs from *Slap Shot*. I
sometimes thought that their fans had seen that film too many
times. They were not good neighbors. The fans of Johnstown
could get as ugly as any in the league.

In my first year in Erie, when Nick was still building the team, we played a nasty game in Johnstown where most of our players were sent to the showers by the third period. In the last couple minutes of the game, we were trying to kill off a five-on-three power play. A fight broke out and the five Johnstown players were beating on our three players. Nick opened the gate and yelled to our bench, "Go, go, go!" Well, I was the only one on the bench still wearing a jersey so, of course, I flew onto the ice. They still had numbers on us so our trainer, Mike Caron, followed me onto the ice and he joined the battle, wearing sweats and street shoes. At one point in the fracas, I looked over to see Mike's bare ass on full display as he wrestled with one of the Wings players. His sweatpants had come down and, unfortunately, he wasn't wearing any drawers. After the fight, Mike was arrested and charged with disturbing the peace. Even Mike would have to admit that "disturbing" was the right word for the show that he put on. Mike spent the night in the Johnstown jail but the charges were eventually dropped after our team paid a fine.

It was not uncommon that the police would be called in to restore order in Johnstown. My teammate Paul Pacific recalls a night when the lawmen had to save some locals who had come hunting for me but wound up biting off more than they could chew.

"Early in a particularly feisty game, I was sent to the locker room and not long afterwards I was joined by Ron Hansis and Val. Ron was a big Texan we called 'Lefty.' He started out skating as a bodyguard on Gordie Howe's line with Houston of the WHA — as if Gordie needed a bodyguard.

"The three of us were alone in the visitor's locker room, talking and joking while the game went on. There was a commotion outside the locker room when about 15 or 20 Johnstown fans showed up at the door. They were drunk and pissed off. They started pounding on the door screaming, 'We're gonna kill you, you fuckin' nigger.' The door was locked so these fans picked up a bench and started to ram the door with it.

"This was different, even for Johnstown. The fans would always yell and throw fishhooks and other things at us but, on this night, we really had a problem. We were seriously outnumbered — and the door wasn't going to hold for long.

"We broke the blades off our hockey sticks and went into the shower. The entrance to the shower was only wide enough for one or two of them to get through at a time so we would be able to keep the numbers more manageable. Our plan was to impale the first ones through the doorway with our broken sticks, that might make the rest of them think twice.

"As the door was being splintered from the outside, one of our fans saw what was happening and he ran and told the Erie bench. The Blades abandoned the ice and ran to the locker room. Our teammates completely devastated the drunks who were trying to get at us. The deputies had their hands full trying to save the locals. It was a mess. The next time we played in Johnstown, they put a steel cage over our bench."

Johnstown was also the first EHL home of supposed tough-guy Bob Phillips. As soon as he arrived in the league, the fans in Johnstown were praising him as the league's new heavyweight champion. I was looking forward to meeting this new champion, who had been given the league's heavyweight belt just for showing up.

Phillips must have believed his own hype. When we first met up on Johnstown's ice, he asked me, "What's a nigger doing trying to play hockey? How about you go play some basketball instead?" I gave him a big smile and responded, "I'll tell you what,

I'm going to show you what I'm doing out here as soon as they drop that puck." The puck was dropped and I dropped Phillips, injuring his shoulder. When we were done, I asked him, "Do you have any more questions for me, Champ?"

Unhappy with the welcome I gave their newest hero, a couple of the more toothless patrons threw nuts and bolts at me. The more dignified of their fans just pelted me with racial slurs.

On another particularly hostile night in Johnstown, a fan threw a live shotgun shell on the ice. We all just stared at it in silence. The fists and the curses and the slurs were a regular part of our Johnstown experience, but this was a different level of threat. Nick put Mike Caron in the penalty box for the rest of the game with his back to the ice so he could watch the crowd.

I don't mean to paint all of the Johnstown fans as cavemen but you tend to remember the ones calling you "nigger" and throwing shit at you. And there was plenty of them in that town. It was not uncommon that our team bus would get a police escort out of Johnstown. "Thanks for stopping by, please do come again."

I came up against Phillips again when he relocated to the Richmond Rifles. He had taken a disliking to one of our most skilled players, Pierre Aubry. Pierre was only 5-foot-10, but by Christmas he led the league in scoring by 35 points. Phillips had six inches and 40 pounds on Pierre so it didn't take much heart for him to go after Aubry every chance he got. My job was to make sure he paid a high price for running our kids. It wasn't easy because Phillips always had plenty of time for guys like Aubry but little time for me. His teammate, Ray Kurpis, often sacrificed himself to keep me from killing Phillips.

Other than Mike Stothers, there was probably no player I fought more than Ray Kurpis. Ray was a strong, tough kid from

Chicago. He was always game and we had some good bouts. Every time we met, we knew we were going to try to punch each other's head off, but there was still a lot of respect between us. We would chat during warm-ups, sometimes planning when we would go during the game but always with the understanding that events during the night could move up fight time at any point.

My first year in Erie, Ray played for Utica. Utica was another unfriendly place to visit. The most cordial of their fans was a pair of identical twin brothers who sat behind the visitor's penalty box during every game. They had bright red hair and each of them topped 300 pounds. These oversized fashion plates always wore matching flannel shirts with greasy coveralls. When you were sent to the box, Dumb and Dumber would be waiting with their signature chant. The first guy would singsong, "Hot-dog!" Then the other genius would follow, "Mus-tard!" As best said by another EHL tough guy, Brent Gogol, these twins definitely made a wrong turn on the set of *Deliverance*. Still, theirs was the friendliest reception I could hope for when the schedule brought us to Utica.

That first year, when Ray Kurpis was in Utica, we were in their building one night and we lined up against each other. Before the puck was dropped, the crowd started chanting "Nigger" at me. It was loud and clear. As often happened in those moments, time seemed to stand still. With the slur echoing throughout the arena, Ray just looked down at the ice and said, "I'm sorry you got to listen to that garbage, Val."

Later, when Ray played in Richmond, he and I hooked up during a bench-clearing brawl in their place. The fight started when our guy Stan Gulutzan went at it with Lawrie Nisker of Richmond during a line change. The gates to the benches were open for the line change so everyone just poured out onto the ice. Many nights when the benches emptied, I had a problem finding a willing partner. As my old teammate Paul Mancini remembers, "Val would be skating around the ice looking for someone to take him on and the other team's players would all be skating away and looking for someone else to pair off with. No one would want to hook up with him, but I would have three players grabbing me, anything to avoid pairing off with Val. I was a real popular guy when that stuff broke out." You could always count on Ray — he was always willing.

Ray and I were really throwing bombs that night in Richmond. At one point, we were going at it so fiercely that the other players stopped fighting to watch us. Paul Pacific was one of these players. "I was ringside for some serious battles but none were better than that one Val and Kurpis had in Virginia. They were connecting with shots that would put down a buffalo."

Of course, my buddy PP has me winning on a late KO but how does Ray remember it? I will let him pick up the story from here. "I hit Val 10 times in the head as hard as I could throw them. Val kept coming, he was just throwing them right back at me. At one point, we both fell face-first to the ice. People tell me I won that one because I landed more punches than he did. But I also went to the hospital because my nose was shattered. I needed to have a steel plate put in my face."

Stan Gulutzan hurt his shoulder in that brawl. While he was in the ER at Richmond General, a stream of ambulances dropped off a bunch of other players from both teams, including Ray. There were seven players in the ER, still wearing their team uniforms, and the police were called to check in because the hospital wasn't sure if the fighting was over. It was. Stan tells us what happened at the hospital. "Kurpis's nose was twisted right over to his ear. I asked him, 'Hey, Ray, what the hell happened to you?' He said, 'It was Val, Stan. I swear I thought I finally had him and then the lights went out.'"

That was a good fight, but I'm not ready to concede defeat in that one. After all, when it was over, I wasn't the one who needed surgery.

About three weeks later, Richmond came to play in Erie. Another line brawl broke out and, of course, Ray and I wound up squaring off. Ray remembers, "I still had the black eyes from our last fight and Val suggests, 'Hey, Ray, why don't we throw a few and then we both can take the rest of the night off?' I agreed but I told him, 'Just don't hit my nose.' He promised and we both threw some shots. Val kept his word and stayed away from my nose. The refs broke things up but the rosters only had 14 players back then, so they couldn't throw everyone out of the game. They made an arbitrary cut of who was getting tossed. I was sent off and Val stayed in. So much for his idea of getting the rest of the night off."

Another Richmond tough guy was Gilles "Bad News" Bilodeau, something of a legendary fighter for Birmingham of the WHA and Quebec of the WHA and NHL. We were told that when Bilodeau played for the Beauce Jaros of the NAHL, his contract stipulated that he receive a $500 bonus every time he drew blood from an opponent. Word had also gotten around that Bilodeau had "gone Dracula" on an opponent, chomping down on his adversary's neck during a scrap. Well, the Count and I hooked up in the second of two games that we played in Richmond one weekend. We had made the trip with only our backup goalie after our starter was injured earlier in the week. Late in the Friday night game, our backup-turned-starter injured his thumb. When he showed up the next day wearing a cast, Nick Polano told our trainer, Mike Caron, to put on the goalie equipment for the first time since he was in high school 10 years earlier. I was on defense that night and I decided that it was my mission to destroy anyone who came too close to my housemate Mike and his goal crease.

As the one-game goaltending wonder recalls, "Bilodeau brushed me during the game and Val launched into him. Bilodeau was built of brick but Val knocked his teeth out. Literally."

I expected a tougher fight. I grabbed him and he tried to turtle. When guys did that, I'd step back, which would give me room for a clean uppercut. I caught him in the mouth and felt some of his teeth break free from his gums. When I would land a good uppercut, I knew the head was going to shoot right up so I'd already be throwing a right cross as his face entered my sights. Many times, that would be the knockout shot. And it was for Bilodeau. That fight was over in seconds.

That was one of three fights I had that night. I was eventually tossed out of the game. We lost the game, but I was proud of Mike who gave up only four goals and made 35 saves.

We also had the occasion to get up close and personal with some of Richmond's fans. One night, Lou Sleigher, one of our players, was injured, so he was in the press box doing the color commentary for the radio broadcast. Lou was only about 5-foot-10, but he was 210 pounds of muscle. I got in a fight along the boards and was beating on a Richmond player when the fans reached over and started swiping at me. Lou ran down from the press box in his street clothes and started fighting with the fans. Our guys saw that Lou was outnumbered so we jumped into the stands to come to his rescue.

Just as the boards didn't always separate the players from the fans, the wall between the penalty boxes didn't always keep the combatants apart. One night, I took exception to something done by Alan Globensky of the New Hampshire Freedom. Al had been around a while, building a rep in juniors as a solid fighter and getting some games with the Quebec Nordiques of the WHA. I knew our trainer Mike was friends with Al, but I didn't know much else about him other than he had one of those cool 1970s afros. I can't remember what he did to piss me off that night but it was enough that I was still unsatisfied when the refs broke up our minor skirmish on the ice.

Sometimes, it is better to let the boys work out their aggression. And that was the case on this night. I was stewing in the penalty box and I could hear Al running his mouth on the other side of the plywood that separated each team's box. I grabbed the plywood and tore it out of its anchoring. Al had a look of shock on his face. We went at it in there but it really wasn't close. I destroyed him. I then headed off to the locker room while the arena staff set about rebuilding the penalty box that we had just demolished.

New Hampshire was also the one-time home of another enforcer, Paul Stewart, with whom I became quite friendly. Yes, a lot of us actually were quite friendly. Despite the fact that part of my job was to kick the piss out of the other team's tough guys, I had a good relationship and rapport with most of those guys. I respected their jobs and their roles because mine was the same.

Stewie was one seriously tough guy that I always respected. Before he became one of the greatest NHL refs of all time, he was a hard-nosed enforcer. He took on a ton of tough guys including Terry O'Reilly, Stan Jonathan, Jack Carlson, Frank Beaton, and many others, not to mention several dust-ups that he and Nicky Fotiu had during one Rangers camp back in the mid-1970s.

Stewie and I went at it a couple of times my first year in Erie when he played for New Hampshire. After the first fight, he had two black eyes and a black ear. In the second fight, we got in a clinch and, pointing at his black ear, I quipped, "Hey Stewie, have you seen your face? I think you're turning black." Without skipping a beat, he responded, "Yeah, well you better check your hands, Val, I think your paint is coming off."

The press asked Stewie after the game for his take on the fights that he had that night. He said, "Well, when the game ended, I had two black eyes that I know I didn't have when the game started." Stewie was as good as you can meet in that business.

Unfortunately, not all friendships survived the rough stuff on the ice. Bob Beatty was a guy I played with and became friends with during senior hockey in Sioux City. He also played with us for a while in Erie during my first year there. He then went on to play for just about every other team in the EHL. Bob was always a willing fighter. His problem was that he was a bleeder. One night, when Bob was with the Hampton Aces, he wanted to go with me. I said, "Bob, you know this isn't going to end well." Bob pushed the issue and I wound up rag-dolling him. I was disappointed that the fight seemed to end our friendship, at least from his side. I knew better than anyone why he needed to fight me. It was his job. But he should have known I had the same job. I just did my job. Still, for the most part, I like to think that the respect and friendships continued after we picked our gloves back up off the ice.

With all the rough stuff that dominated the Eastern Hockey League, you might be surprised by some of the people who got their start there. And not just players like me, or coaches like Nick

Polano, or broadcasters like JP Dellacamera. Patrick Meehan is a well-regarded United States Congressman from Pennsylvania, but before his successful career in public service, first as a criminal prosecutor and now as an elected representative of the people, Pat was a well-regarded hockey referee. We first crossed paths when we were both rookies in the EHL, me with the Erie Blades and Pat wearing the striped shirt. Pat later worked many of the games I played in the AHL. His recent recollection of his first game in the EHL paints an accurate picture of what life was like in "the E" in those days.

"My first pro game as a ref was at the Erie Coliseum with the Blades playing the Baltimore Clippers. Nicky Polano was the Blades' coach and he was very competitive. It was the home opener for Erie and the start of the new season. Just before play was to begin, the two wingers behind me started to jostle one another so I stepped in and separated them. I got ready to drop the puck but these two started at each other again. So I stopped them again. The third time, they moved on to pushing each other. Then they dropped the gloves and started swinging. The other two wingers did the same, dropping their gloves too. Suddenly, Erie's goalie skated towards center ice and the Baltimore goalie skated over to meet him. Then both benches emptied. There were 32 guys wrestling and fighting on the ice, and the game hadn't even started. The Erie crowd was going crazy. All of this before I dropped the puck for my first game as a pro ref."

Pat's experience as a referee in the brawling days of the EHL probably comes in handy in his current job. After all, who is better suited for sorting out all those battles they have on the floor of Congress?

Put 'em all in the penalty box, Pat!

NINETEEN

FOR ALL OF HIS MANY ATTRIBUTES, Jackie Robinson's most extraordinary traits were the grace and restraint he displayed in the face of constant racial abuse. His response to the vile taunting that followed him wherever he played was to turn the other cheek. In my case, however, too much of that kind of self-control would not have been seen as a sign of strength. A non-threatening image would hardly be an asset to a hockey enforcer — I could only be effective if I was feared. For me, turning the other cheek would mean a one-way ticket back to Long Island.

When the racist insults came from the mouth of an opponent, I had a ready response: I would crack the guy's skull. Ray Kurpis recently spoke about running into one of his old Utica teammates at a reunion. This player recalled trying to agitate me by calling me a nigger. He told Ray, "I agitated him all right. And I still have the bumps on my head that Val gave me for opening my mouth."

I had a very short fuse when it came to a fellow hockey player disrespecting me like that. None of them was getting a free pass. It was much more difficult to respond, however, when the racism came from another team's fans.

111

In the Eastern Hockey League, racial harassment from the crowds was a regular part of my gig. I knew that some sort of ugliness was waiting for me at the end of each long bus ride. The last miles before we reached our destination, my teammates would start getting focused, visualizing their play in the upcoming game. I did the same. But my own mental preparation included consideration of the slurs that were waiting for me when I hit the ice. I had to ready myself for the attacks and prepare for how I would respond and how I would not.

Going into the stands to personally deliver a lesson on civility to a drunken inbred was the option that came most naturally, and felt the best, but it also cost the most. Brawling with fans, no matter how racist, would always result in a suspension and a fine, maybe a lawsuit as well. It might also scare off potential NHL suitors. Still, nothing releases rage like making a racist eat his filthy words.

I did wonder how much some people would have to hate their own lives in order to feel the need to degrade me. I supposed that the chanting and cursing was the only way that they could forget their own sorry existence and feel superior to someone else for a few minutes. Pal, your world must be pretty pathetic if your only joy comes from hiding in a crowd and cursing someone else just because of the color of that person's skin. Now, don't get me wrong, the pity I felt for these losers did not lessen either my fury or my desire to feed them my hockey stick. Still, I expect that I would have run out of sticks long before I ran out of racist mouths to fill.

It didn't matter which town we were in. Johnstown, Utica, and Baltimore were all north of the Mason-Dixon line, but they could hold their own with the racial abuse dished out in the more southern towns where we played, such as Salem, Richmond, and Hampton. All of these places had more than enough racists who figured that paying three or four bucks for a ticket entitled them to drop in after work and curse out the black guy.

The chanting of "nigger" or "coon" or "spear chucker" were sometimes the loudest chants of the night. In Utica, whole sections of fans chanted "nigger" throughout some games. In Johnstown, some fans made and held up posters of me dressed in stereotypical African garb, with a grass skirt and a bone through my nose, holding a spear. Other fans would wave fried chicken at me. The worst, however, probably came in Salem, Virginia.

In the early months of 1981, I was told that the news program, *CBS News Sunday Morning* with Charles Kuralt, wanted to do a story on the black kid trying to make it in the all-white sport of ice hockey. My journey probably sounded to them like the makings of a nice human-interest piece for Mr. Kuralt's "On the Road" segment of the broadcast. Since the news bureau was in Washington, D.C., the crew waited until we came in to Virginia for a weekend series against the Salem Raiders.

Any idea that CBS had for taping a feel-good tale went out the window when I took to the ice at the Salem-Roanoke County Civic Center. With the news camera rolling, the crowd immediately started chanting, "Spook . . . Spook . . . Spook . . ." It went on the whole night. They also filmed a number of individual fans in all their racist glory, including one pimply teenage boy who held up a watermelon with my name on it. Other images captured that night were racist fathers out for a night with their kids, yelling out "nigger" each time I passed, teaching their young children all about hockey and hatred.

Of course, there were always many fans who did not join in

the abuse. Now and again, I would receive a letter from folks who wanted to apologize for what the others had made me endure in their towns. Still, the racist fans made the most noise and they faced little risk of being kicked out for their behavior. Their hoods might have been white, but the cash they laid out to buy their tickets was green.

When word got out that CBS would be filming in Salem, the arena did make an announcement at the start of that game, saying that the use of offensive language was prohibited. Mr. Kuralt suggested calling it "the Val James rule." It might better have been called "the CBS rule" because the arena had never made that announcement before the news people showed up. Either way, neither the announcement nor the presence of news cameras could stop the slurs and, as usual, not a single soul got tossed out for playing the racist fool. So the decent people who just wanted to bring their families to a hockey game also had to be exposed to the disgraceful attacks aimed my way.

Since I couldn't act on my fantasy of shoving a hockey puck down the throat of every big-mouthed racist, one acceptable way for me to respond to these attacks was to turn up my physical play. If I could knock one of their hometown players into next week, then some of my anger might fade. I had players on these southern teams approach me during the pregame skate and tell me that they weren't looking for any problems with me but the booster clubs demanded that they take on "Erie's black guy." These guys were hoping to limit the fury I would unleash on them later that night, but their own fans often drove me in the other direction and I took it out on their players. Sorry, boys.

I did have an opportunity for a free shot at one of my tormentors during a road trip to one of the southern cities. I had gotten into a scrap on the ice and I was in the penalty box, serving a major for fighting. As usual, I was being taunted by a fan yelling slurs into the box. This particular slob leaned closer and closer, calling me every racist name in the hillbilly handbook. I just glanced at him and then turned away, shaking my head. Still not satisfied, Captain Courageous then tossed his beer on me: a bull's eye. I jumped up, but I didn't follow him as he hauled his fat ass up the stairs and out of harm's way. After the game, our team was unwinding in the hotel bar when, by coincidence, I saw the beer thrower. He didn't see me as I quietly approached. "So, pal, do you want to throw your drink on me now?" The guy looked up and turned ghost white when he saw me towering over him. He stammered an apology before taking off, happy to escape with nothing more than shitted drawers.

It took little courage, and less brains, to bombard me with racial slurs from the safety of the bleachers. I knew I wasn't going to be able to change their minds. Unfortunately, I wouldn't be able to kick their asses either, as long as I wanted to keep playing hockey. And I wasn't going to let them force me out of the game I loved.

While my opponents knew very well that I was not one to turn the other cheek, I had no choice but to swallow the abuse hurled at me from their fans. To the haters, I was an easy target. My skin was dark. My hair was kinky. There was no mistaking me for a white guy with a tan. Big and black, I was the bogeyman to these cowardly racists. There was no one else in the building that looked like me, either on the ice or in the stands. As a black man in a white sport, I was all by myself.

TWENTY

MY DAD HAD BEEN TO Cherry Hill, New Jersey, to see me play my first exhibition game with the Erie Blades. I think it was the last game he ever saw me play. His duties at the Long Island Arena kept him busy seven days a week. We would talk regularly by telephone but he never did make it to Erie.

I was fortunate that my two younger brothers came to stay with me from time to time in Erie, sometimes with my mom and sometimes on their own. They would stay with me and my house-mates, who always welcomed my family as if they were their own.

My brothers weren't yet in their teens, so they could be a handful. One night while my brother Robert was staying with us, I came home to find him bouncing off the walls. He was so wild that I thought something might be medically wrong with him. My own life passed before my eyes because Robert was my mother's youngest. "You take good care of my baby, Valmore. Don't you take your eyes off him, do you understand?"

Despite my mother's warning, I had slipped out of the house and came back to find Robert running around from room to room, carrying on like a madman. Before calling 9-1-1, I went in the kitchen and found that Robert had just eaten a full king-sized box of Cap'n Crunch cereal. The sugar had sent him into orbit, but it was nothing I couldn't cure with a couple of hockey sticks and a roll of hockey tape. I taped Robert to the sticks and left him propped against the wall until the sugar wore off. My brother Hank also came to visit, but he didn't cause any problems, beyond eating all our food.

Mike Caron remembers a time when my mom and Hank both came for a visit. "Val was scared of the dark . . ."

There he goes with that again.

"Val was scared of the dark and he would go to sleep with the lights on and a blanket pulled up over his head. I came home late one night and saw Val, his mom, and Hank, all of them had fallen asleep on the couch while watching television. All the lights in the house were turned on and the three of them had a single blanket pulled up over their heads while they snoozed."

I treasured the times when my family could come see me play in Erie. My folks had given up plenty for me to be able to play hockey. But they weren't alone in their sacrificing on my behalf: There were six kids in our family, and each of the others had to do without something every time that the few dollars we did have were spent on some hockey equipment or a hockey camp for me. I was proud of my team in Erie and of my own hockey skills. I had become a much better player and I hoped my family was proud of what I had accomplished as a result of their sacrifice and support all those years.

But the great times I had in Erie were soon to come to a close. So too was the most important relationship of my life.

During my last season with the Blades, my dad was diagnosed with cancer. He opted for surgery but the disease spread throughout his body, lightning quick and without mercy.

A few years earlier, my dad had been in a horrible car accident in Upstate New York. The Long Island Cougars had just played, and lost, a playoff game in Binghamton. My dad had driven to the game and brought along Joan McCann, one of the administrative folks in the front office at the arena; Joan's teenage daughter; Lenny Gagnon, who was the referee-in-chief for NAHL; and Artie Powers, the vendor in charge of concessions at the arena. On the way home, there was a tractor trailer stopped on the highway. My dad didn't see the truck on the dark road, and they crashed full speed into the back of the rig. Lenny and Artie were killed instantly. Joan and her daughter were severely injured. My dad took a bad beating. He went to the memorial services while covered in bandages, deeply distraught. All of these people were part of my dad's arena family. I don't think he ever forgave himself for what happened. I believe that part of him felt he should have died that night too.

When my dad got sick, he lost a lot of weight. He was always known as a big, powerful man and his body was decimated. At one point, he dropped below 90 pounds. He didn't want people to come see him in the hospital. He wanted to be remembered the way he was before he got sick.

Shortly before my dad died, I got a contract offer from the Buffalo Sabres organization. Nick Polano had been hired as Scotty Bowman's assistant in Buffalo and he recommended that Scotty give me a shot. My dad and I held that contract and wept. Together we had dreamed of the day I would sign a pro contract and that day finally came. Now, I would have to face the future without him.

TWENTY-ONE

I KNEW FROM MY BRIEF STAY with the Red Wings that rookies like myself had no real chance of being noticed at the big club's camp before being sent down for a look from the farm team. It was no different when I arrived at the Sabres camp for the 1981–82 pre-season. I skated in a few circles with Buffalo before getting shipped out to the Rochester Americans camp. My stay in the NHL camp was brief, but I can't say that I went completely unnoticed.

Nick Polano had convinced Sabres GM and legendary Canadiens coach Scotty Bowman to sign me to the organization. Nick told Scotty that I could ably fill the role of peacemaker for the team, a role I had played for Nick in Erie. On Nick's word alone, Scotty gave me a contract. The first day I took to the ice at the Sabres camp, Scotty ran up to Nick. "Hey Nick, did you know there's a big black guy out there?" Nick hadn't thought to mention to Scotty that I was black. I was never one to exactly "blend in" on a hockey rink anyway. So, you might say that I did manage to get noticed in my first camp with the Sabres.

Nick was my champion with the Buffalo organization, as he had been during my time in Erie. Still, there was no guaranteed spot for me in Rochester. Nick was able to get me an opportunity to prove that I belonged; the rest was entirely on me. After the disaster of the Detroit camp a few years earlier, I was determined to make a positive impression this time around. I also knew that this truly was my last shot. Nick encouraged me, "Just play your game, Val. If you kick a few asses the way you did in Erie, you'll turn some heads."

I already had some familiarity with the Rochester Americans from a three game call-up I had during the previous season, my last year in Erie. I was a mid-season roster fill-in and I got a taste of the increased speed and size of the American Hockey League. It was also an opportunity to test my fighting ability at this advanced level. In a game at the Hershey Arena, I challenged Archie Henderson of the Bears to a fight. Archie was already a league legend and he had nothing to gain by accepting my invitation, but he was gracious enough to give me a shot. An up-and-coming fighter has to depend on the willingness of the established fighters to give the new guy a chance to show off his skills. There were plenty of so-called "tough guys" who forgot where they came from and considered fighting rookies to be beneath them. Of course, these guys preferred to cherry-pick their opponents and pad their penalty minutes, while avoiding any real challenges by hiding behind their seniority. I vowed that, once I established myself, I would give every new jack his fair chance to prove himself too.

Archie was an honorable man and he gave me my chance. I'm not sure if he soon regretted his hospitality. I quickly landed a couple of glancing blows to his head and I think that was enough for him. He pulled me into a tight bear hug to end the bout.

Jim Doyle was the referee for that game in Hershey. Jim

recently shared his recollection of my fight with Archie. "I let Archie and Val fight until they were tired and then I stepped in. As they separated, Archie tapped Val on the head and said, 'Hey kid, you did a great job. You just went with one of the best.'"

Archie was right. And I was grateful that he gave me the chance to show I had the willingness and the ability to go with the league's best.

When I arrived at my first camp with Rochester, I met the team's head coach, Mike Keenan. Mike was just starting his second season with the Americans. They had finished in last place and out of the playoffs the previous year. The team was still a work in progress and Mike wasn't the most patient guy in the world. I knew I didn't have a lot of time if I wanted to make the roster when we broke camp. I wanted to show Mike and the rest of the team that I was a guy they could depend on when things got rough on the ice.

Our team trainer, Jim Pizzutelli, mentioned to me that Don Gillen of the Binghamton Whalers was thought to be the toughest fighter in the league. Pizza hinted that beating Gillen would go a long way towards me landing a spot with the club. As luck would have it, our pre-season schedule included an exhibition game against Binghamton. As soon as we hit the ice, Gillen started running his mouth. I understood what he was trying to do. I was brand new in the league and he was trying to intimidate me, trying to make me doubt myself. I might have been new to the AHL but I wasn't new to the game, or to brawling.

Once Gillen had finally talked himself out, I spoke up. "Oh yeah, that's right, I think I heard of you. You're supposed to be good at this fighting stuff. Well, I see you are pretty good at talking shit, that's for sure. What do you say that when they drop the puck, we see how good you really are?" We squared off and he started with a few soft jabs before moving on to bigger bombs. Unfortunately for him, he threw those haymakers at a snail's pace. While he was winding up, I was hammering him. He was swinging at where I had been and I was throwing them to where he was going. I dazed him with a blast right on the button. He immediately abandoned all thoughts of offense as I followed up with a few lesser blows until he grabbed me, trying to hang on until the refs could come to the rescue. The fight wasn't even close. I was in the AHL to stay.

I met a number of guys at that first camp who I would play with for years. One of my new teammates was Malcolm Davis. Mal was a scary good skater and he was surprised to be bumped down from the Sabres camp to play an Americans pre-season exhibition against New Brunswick. This was a pretty clear sign to Mal that he was not going to make the Sabres opening night roster. Mal was in a bad mood and, during the game, he got in a fight with Alain "Bam Bam" Belanger of New Brunswick. Belanger was not a guy I would have suggested that Mal take a swipe at. I had fought him a bunch of times in the QHL when I was on the Quebec Remparts and he played for Sherbrooke. I always felt that he was one of the toughest fighters in the Q. He was a lefty, which caught me by surprise the first time around. I think I got the better of him in all our fights, but I'll always remember him for giving me my first black eye. As they say, you never forget your first!

Before the exhibition in Rochester, Alain and I caught up for a few minutes during warm-ups. Before we parted ways, I told him, "You know we're gonna have to do this again tonight, Alain." He understood. He was a pro.

Mal and Belanger were mismatched so I kept a close eye on

them from the bench. It didn't get too out of hand so I stayed put. As Mal recalls, "I wasn't known for dropping my gloves so I think Bam Bam was surprised because he took it easy on me. We went to the penalty box and when the penalty expired, Val was waiting for Belanger. Of course, Val handled him from there."

Breaking training camp, I was excited about my new team. We had talent and we were starting to develop some grit. We had a smart, demanding coach. I liked our chances.

That first season I spent in Rochester was positive for me and for the team. Coach Keenan preached the concept of team success built upon the execution of each individual's role. We had several guys who could fill the net and several more who could clear space for the scorers to ply their trade. The league was loaded with tough guys and I introduced myself to so many of them that I spent better than 200 minutes in the penalty box. The American Hockey League in the mid-1980s played as rugged a game of hockey as any in history. Guys like myself, Chris Langevin, and Don Keller brought real value to the Americans beyond scoring goals. I had five goals in 65 games that season, but my true contribution was better measured by the effect I could have on my teammates and their game.

A team might have the most talent in the league, but it's meaningless if their top players are being smacked and hacked every time they're on the ice. My friend Geordie Robertson was one of the snipers on our Americans team. He recently remarked, "Val and Chris Langevin turned me from a benchwarmer into the guy setting the scoring record for the franchise. That was no coincidence. They gave me space. I could focus on my job, which was scoring goals."

There was no pretense about what my role was on the team.

Our opponents would only take advantage of our skilled players to the extent that there were no consequences for doing so. Mike put me on the team to establish those consequences in the minds of our opponents. I'm confident I succeeded in my job. Mike still says, "Val kept the other teams honest. His presence was a serious deterrent. He mastered his role better than any player in the AHL. There were a lot of tough players in the league back then. A lot of heavyweights. Val James was the best of all the heavyweights in the league. No one was tougher."

Just as each of the players had their roles, Coach Keenan had his role too. Most days we thought his role was to bust our balls. Turns out, breaking balls was not his role, it was just his favorite method of motivating us. Mike's role was to make sure that we knew *our* roles and that we performed them with maximum effort. Nothing else was acceptable.

Mike was the perfect coach for the "take no prisoners" style of hockey played in the AHL back then. When we went on the road, Mike's attitude was, "Let's eat all their food and fuck all their women." I figured that he must have been a Viking commander in a prior life.

Mike also enjoyed getting his nose dirty in our intra-squad scrimmages. He would lace up his skates and play for one team or the other. He was a complete pest out there. A master agitator. Mike really could have given Kenny Linseman a run for the title of "king of the ball busters." He would bump you, poke you, and chirp in your ear. Like Linseman, you would want to take his head off. Some of the guys did knock him around a lot. Mark Wichrowski got a kick out of "accidentally" dropping Mike a few times. Hell, we all got a kick out of it. After all, when do you ever get a free shot to put your boss on his ass like that? Still, Mike always bounced back for more. I think he thrived on it.

While Mike became one of the biggest supporters I had in my career, I suspect that all that heavy punching I did during our first season together made him a little unsure about his new enforcer. Mike did not have an assistant coach in Rochester so Pizza, our trainer, was Mike's confidant and unofficial assistant coach. During that first year, our team started to click and I mentioned to Pizza that I would like to see more time on the ice. He said that he would arrange a sit-down between me and Mike.

Pizza tells me that he then went to Keenan: "Mike, you need to talk to Val. We always say how important he is to our team, even when he's on the bench. All the other teams say, 'Let the giant sleep.' Our guys can play their game knowing that the other guys see Val there, ready to jump over the boards. So, you need to make sure he knows how we feel."

Keenan agreed to bring me into his office for a chat, but he said that he wanted Pizza to be there for the meeting. Pizza told him, "I'm not going in there, Mike. You're the coach, he needs to hear from you one-on-one."

In the War Memorial Arena, the coach's office had only one way in and one way out. So I would be sitting between Mike and the door and he wondered how he might get past me if he needed to escape in a hurry. Keenan pleaded with Pizza, "But what if Val gets pissed off at me?"

Since Pizza and I had a close relationship from the beginning, Pizza told Keenan that he would climb up into the ceiling tiles of the office and, if he heard anything getting out of control, he would just drop in and calm me down.

The meeting with Mike went well, and I didn't find out until 30 years later that Pizza was up there the whole time.

We finished my first season with the Americans in second place in our division. Our total of 89 points was an improvement of 21 points over the team's performance the previous year. We got past the New Haven Nighthawks in the first round of the playoffs, but we fell to our downstate rivals, the Binghamton Whalers, in the next. Still, our success that year brought us closer as a team and gave us greater confidence going forward. That taste of the playoffs only made us hungry for more the following season.

TWENTY-TWO

THE 1981–82 SEASON WAS also when my impossible hockey dream finally came true. It had been barely 10 years since my dad had given me my first pair of skates as an early 13th birthday present. For most of that decade, he and I were the only people who even dreamed out loud that I might someday play in the world's greatest hockey league. Since losing my old man the previous year, I was left to carry on that dream for the both of us.

I knew from talking to Pizza that the organization was happy with my play in Rochester. Through his relationship with Keenan, Pizza was plugged in to the thoughts and intentions of the front office. Late in the season, Pizza pulled me aside at practice and gave me the news that I thought might never come. "You're being called up by Buffalo, Val. Go show them what you can do." He reminded me, "Don't forget what got you there. Go kick some serious ass like you did down here."

It didn't take long to travel the 70 miles from Rochester to Buffalo but, at the same time, it was a journey that had taken a lifetime. I was happier and prouder than I had ever been. My only regret was that I couldn't share those feelings with my dad.

I did have some butterflies as I prepared to take this big step. I was completely fine with the idea of fighting guys at the top level. I had already fought many former and current NHL tough guys and that was just another day at the office for me. My case of the nerves came from the higher level of hockey skill that I knew I would be facing. In particular, I knew I had to put my skating up against the best in the world. These guys had been skating since they could walk. They were on the ice for 10 years before I ever got my first pair of skates. I just didn't want to embarrass myself.

My first game in the NHL was against the Philadelphia Flyers in the old Buffalo Memorial Auditorium. My friend Robin Roberts Jr., a former broadcaster for the Erie Blades, drove to Buffalo to see my debut. "As I entered the Aud, I saw Val in the lobby. He was very excited and he couldn't believe how much more money he would make while he was called up. I sat in the press box and, before the game, an old-time hockey writer from Philadelphia asked me for some background on Val. I mentioned that he was an American player from New York, and he was a tough guy on a bunch of championship teams in Erie. The players then skated out and the reporter almost choked on his cigar when he saw Val. Val is very dark skinned and the Sabres home jerseys were predominantly white, bright white. The reporter shouted out, 'He's black? You didn't tell me that!'"

I sat on the bench for most of the game. In the last minute or two of the third period, Nick Polano told me to take a spin. When my skates hit the ice, I was aware that I had just become the first black American to ever play in the National Hockey League. Still, that wasn't my first thought. As I skated in my first NHL game, my mind turned immediately to my dad and how proud he must be, looking down on me at that very moment. He had been right. He encouraged me through all the practices and bus trips, all the disappointments and doubts. I thought of all the sacrifices made by my whole family. It all led to this night. We really did it, Pop.

The Buffalo fans knew me from Rochester and they applauded my turn on the ice. There was no special announcement or official acknowledgment of the moment, either then or since. But it didn't matter. I knew. And I knew that somewhere the old man knew too.

On the ice, Kenny Linseman took a run at me along the boards. He bumped me with what he must have thought was a hard check. "The Rat," as he was known, bounced right off me and I turned and stared down at him. He didn't have the heart to take it any further and he skated off while he still could.

During my time in Buffalo, there were a number of games where I skated in the warm-up but did not get off the bench during the game. This was the case in Montreal and New York. I did get in a game in Quebec and some of my friends from my QHL days came to see me play. I rang a shot off the post behind their goalie, Richard Sevigny, missing my chance at a first NHL goal by *just that much.*

My Sabres career was brief, but the highlights probably came during a pair of games we played against the Boston Bruins. Buffalo played in a very physical conference in those days. Some of the games against their rival from Boston had seen the Sabres bullied by the Big Bad Bruins, led by their feisty veteran Terry O'Reilly. When Nick Polano recommended to Scotty Bowman that I get called up, it was to give Terry the fight he always seemed to be itching for. "O'Reilly had taken some liberties with our team. Val was brought up specifically to deal with him. And that's what he did."

We first played the Bruins in a road game at the Garden. The

Sabres had spent that whole year getting out muscled by Boston. Scotty's game plan was for us to meet, even exceed, their level of physical play. In case there were any doubts as to his intentions, he put me on a line with Lindy Ruff and Larry Playfair. This was a line intended to deliver a whole lot of nastiness. And that we did. We banged everything in sight and took on all comers. In one scrap, I made short work of one of the Crowder boys. I didn't have enough time to feed him anything more than a few lefts, but it was more than enough. When the second brother came calling, I told him that he might want to think twice. "You don't want your momma crying over both her boys tonight, do you?" Unfortunately, O'Reilly did not play that night, as he was out nursing an injury. We didn't win the game but we did make the statement that Scotty and Nick had intended. Win or lose, we were going to go out on our feet.

As we sat on the team bus outside the Boston Garden, I thought again about how far I had come. I had just finished playing, and contributing, in an NHL game at an Original Six arena. It had taken years to reach this point but I knew I had to savor the moment because no one could say how long it would last. Still, on this night, I was going to allow myself just a moment to bask in the pride that came from making it to this point in my career. Unfortunately, the moment passed too quickly. I suppose I should have known better than to let my guard down.

As I sat on the bus, replaying the game in my mind, a loud crash snapped me back to reality. I looked up to see the front windshield had been splintered by a beer bottle. A crowd of Bruins fans gathered in front of the bus. They were obviously less impressed with my performance than I had been. They started shouting, "Send out the nigger!" I stood up and started towards the front of the bus but Scotty told me to sit back down. I returned to my seat, trying to hide the tears that had started to flow from my eyes. My teammates looked away, pretending that they hadn't noticed me crying.

We drove off and I immediately regretted not getting off that bus. My fists throbbed with adrenaline. Those drunks had taken away the joy and pride I had felt at achieving a lifelong dream. They had insulted me and embarrassed me in front of my team. They had challenged me, both as a man and as a black man. They had assaulted me, physically by throwing the bottle and verbally with the lowest of fighting words. I wanted to tear their little lynch mob to shreds. Instead, we drove away, with the fury still eating at my gut. A week later, I was able to release some of that rage.

The Bruins were now in Buffalo for a game on our ice. I finally got to meet up with the leader of the Bruins, Terry O'Reilly. We didn't have to wait long to get down to business. A few minutes into the first period, Terry and I lined up across from one another and waited for a faceoff. We dropped our gloves just as the puck hit the ice. It was another quick fight but this time it was my right hand that shortened the length of the bout. I caught Terry with a couple of those rights and down he went. The icing in that game was that we treated our home fans to a win over the hated Bruins.

I know O'Reilly complained to the press after the game that the Sabres had brought me up for the sole purpose of fighting him. His comment was the only validation I needed that I had been effective. I had done what was expected of me.

TWENTY-THREE

MY SECOND SEASON WITH ROCHESTER started much like my first. I made a brief appearance at the Sabres camp before heading to the Americans camp. Besides our own high expectations for the coming year, the fans of Rochester were also excited about the 1982–83 season. It had been 15 years since the Americans had last won the AHL's championship, the Calder Cup. People thought this could very well be the year that we got it done.

Rochester's fans were very proud of their team and their town, and rightfully so. JC Ihrig, now a big shot for Reebok, was the stick boy for the Americans back then. JC was a local kid and he recently described his hometown this way, "There was a lot of pride in our town. We had IBM, we had Kodak, we had Xerox. And we had the Americans. We were New York. Buffalo? That was a place where we dumped our garbage. Rochester was where it was at."

As was the practice for decades, the players on our team were welcomed warmly into the community of Rochester. I was no exception. We wanted to justify the strong support given to us by the fans. We wanted to win them that Calder Cup that they were dreaming about.

Unfortunately, the way we started the season was anything but promising. We lost our first three games and, by Thanksgiving, we had managed only eight wins, good enough for sixth place in the Northern Division. This was not the way we expected to begin our year. Coach Keenan was enraged and his practices were not a fun place to be. One of the more miserable sessions was the Thanksgiving Day Massacre, a holiday practice when Mike skated us to the point where we would have gladly traded places with that evening's turkey.

A lot of teams would have completely imploded from such a horrendous start, but our group kept believing that we were much better than our record said we were. A tremendous calming influence in our locker room was veteran Yvon Lambert. Lambert knew how to win and he had the Stanley Cup rings to prove it. After years as a key piece of the Montreal Canadiens' late 1970s dynasty, Yvon had come to our team on a tryout contract. Thankfully, he made the team. Whenever Mike stormed out of the room after he was done ripping us a new one, Yvon filled the silence that followed. He taught us that supporting and encouraging each other during our tough stretch was more important than doing so during the fat times. Nothing could be fixed by infighting and finger-pointing. We had dug the hole as a team and we believed we would dig out of it the same way.

Then, a funny thing happened: the team clicked. Mike had made some personnel adjustments but none were as effective as his move of my housemate Jim Wiemer from forward to defense. The team went on a roll and, by Christmas, we were in first place to stay.

We never let up the rest of the way. We expected to win and, most of the time, we did. Playing at home in Rochester, a victory was all but guaranteed. Despite the good things happening for us, it was pretty obvious that Coach Keenan was not feeling a lot of love from the suits in the front office. Mike could be a maniac sometimes, but he had put together a dominant team and we were heading towards great things. Still, Mike was in the last year of his contract and, from my perspective, it didn't seem that there was any urgency to get him re-signed. It was crazy but I started sensing this could be Mike's last season.

We finished the year with 101 points, the best in the AHL. Our regular season dominance meant that we would have the home rink advantage throughout the playoffs. The first two rounds were tougher than we expected, but the lessons of perseverance that we had learned during our early-season rut came in handy during those games.

In the first series, we lost a hard-fought opening game to our Binghamton rivals before coming back to tie up the series in the second game. Binghamton stepped up the nastiness in Game 3. We responded in kind. We were shorthanded late in the game when a scrum broke out behind the Whalers' net. Their guys decided they would not let the advantage in numbers go to waste. No less than three Binghamton players started pounding on our big Finnish defenseman, Kari Suoraniemi. The assault was led by the Whalers' Dave McDonald, their 6-foot-2, 220-pound enforcer. Seeing this mismatch, Coach Keenan opened the gate to our bench. "Get in there, boys." He did not need to tell us twice.

I led our charge off the bench and I beelined it straight for McDonald. I crashed hard into him and knocked him off the pileup on top of Kari. McDonald's eyes bugged out when he saw that the sides had evened up and he had drawn me as his dance partner. His knees started to buckle before I threw a single punch. He tried to hit the deck before my fist could reach his jaw. My fist won that race and I tagged him twice before he turtled.

We won the battle, and the game, but our coach had to answer to the press after the final buzzer sounded. It was classic Mike Keenan, who told the reporters, "We contained our players on the bench until we finally realized that Binghamton was not going to let up. They outnumbered us by three players at that time. I had no other choice so I sent our bench over. I advised our players to leave the bench and be involved in the fight. It was very calculated, no question about it, but I had no other choice."

No backing down. No denials. No apologies. Amen to that, coach.

Despite Mike's passionate argument that emptying our bench was an act of self-defense, the league suspended only Chris Langevin and Clint Fehr from our side. But we had no regrets. We would always have each other's back. We won the fights, the game, and two wins later, we finished off Binghamton.

In the second round, it took a full seven games to beat back New Hampshire, and not before Jim Wiemer scored double over-time, winning goals in two consecutive games. For my part, I was thrilled at the confidence that Coach Keenan showed in me during the playoffs. I played in some key spots, including during the Finals. Since I had made the team as a fighter, Mike's belief in me during those playoffs was something I was determined not to betray.

Pete Rogers is now the trainer for the Nashville Predators but, back in 1983, he was another one of the stick boys that our trainer Jim Pizzutelli had on his staff. Pete recently said, "Val's role was as an enforcer on the Americans, but he played a fairly regular shift for us in the 1983 playoffs when we won the Calder

Cup. You didn't see many enforcers who were trusted to play in the playoffs and you never see it at all anymore."

Of course, the capper for me came in the last game of the final round. We were playing the Maine Mariners and our team was firing on all cylinders. We won the first three games and took the ice in Maine in Game 4 with a chance to wrap it up. It was a tight game and the Mariners were desperate to avoid a sweep in their own arena. Mike had me on the ice early on. Jim Wiemer kept the Mariners from clearing the puck out of their defensive zone and Mike Moller got a hold of it on the right wing side. Mike threw a pass across the ice to me on the left wing. My buddy Chris Langevin can take it from there. "I can still see Val's goal. Val got the puck at the top of the left circle and took a terrific wrist shot. That was the game-winning goal of the Calder Cup."

Sean McKenna went on a playoff tear for the ages, scoring 14 goals for us during that post-season run. Jean-François Sauvé pitched in 28 points. Some guys had a knack for hitting the net. Usually, I had a knack for hitting the goalie. But not on this night. My goal did indeed wind up being the Calder Cup winner. I had scored the series winner when we won our first championship in Erie and I also scored an important goal when we won the clinching game of the QHL championship in Quebec City. I wasn't known for scoring many goals so I was always thrilled to contribute in that way. I was also honored to hear Coach Keenan say, "It was only fitting that Val scored the game-winning goal in the final game. He was a big part of our championship so it was fun that he was the guy who scored that goal. He deserved it."

We came back to Rochester as champions of the AHL. The airport was mobbed when we touched down. The headline across the front page of the next day's *Rochester Times-Union* newspaper shouted "Crowd Welcomes Triumphant Amerks." The subhead on the same page read "Val James Stars in 3-1 Clincher." The article said, "The Amerks received a solid effort from everyone, especially Val James. The rugged winger, better known for using his fists than his stick, scored his first playoff goal at 13:43 of the first period, which gave the Amerks a 2-0 lead. 'Val James was the key,' Sean McKenna said. 'When he was out there, Maine was afraid. They didn't go near him. When he had the chance to put it in, he did.'"

The City of Rochester held a huge parade for us and I think every man, woman, and child in the town showed up at City Hall for the ceremony. However, the end of that season was bittersweet. We accomplished our goal of winning the Calder Cup but we soon learned that our defense of that championship would have to take place without Coach Keenan. The front office decided to part ways with him not long after the last of the confetti was being swept off the streets.

The next season, 1983–84, Scotty Bowman reached out to the Americans' legendary coach, Joe Crozier, to replace Mike Keenan. Joe was the coach the last time the team had won the Calder Cup, back in 1968. Joe was a rugged old-hockey man, and he took a liking to my style of play. The feeling was mutual.

Joe put me on the first line in Rochester with two of our best goal scorers, Claude Verret and Mal Davis. He told me, "If anyone touches one of your guys, you destroy them." He did not need to tell me twice. Joe said that this assignment would get me called back up to Buffalo by the end of the season. It worked out as well as Joe had planned. Claude and Mal were able to play their game, which made them very dangerous players. And they each knew I had their back. As Mal tells it, "Val's presence made our opponents play an honest game. He had a real calming effect on the other team."

Not all of our opponents got the message that my linemates were off-limits. For instance, one night, we played a road game against the Baltimore Skipjacks. Their up-and-comer, Marty McSorley, ran Claude in front of the Skipjacks' net and knocked him to the ice. I was on McSorley in an instant. I must have popped him with a half-dozen shots right on the kisser, and I didn't catch one in return. It really was no contest.

Joe also thought to invite me to participate in a weekly sports segment, "Crow's Corner," that he used to do on the local news. The broadcast was on WHEC, Channel 10. Each week, Joe would get a couple of Americans players and tape instructional segments on winning faceoffs, killing power plays, and other hockey fundamentals. One week, Joe brought me and Lou Crawford along to teach the kids about fighting. Joe had us show the young ones how to get their arms free and how best to get leverage over their opponents. Then Joe gave them the best possible advice, "The most important thing is to get in the first punch." Of course, the phone lines blew up with complaints from various crybabies. Joe's honest response to the controversy did little to calm down the suits in the league office. He told the press, "Maybe there were 100, 150 callers complaining. But what about the thousands who were hollering for Val James to go at it last weekend?" Joe caught a lot of shit for that program and he had to pay a fine, but his legend only grew larger in the eyes of the Rochester players and fans.

Needless to say, Joe treated me very well — even after I broke his arm. Jim Pizzutelli recalls, "During practice, Val was skating and looked down for a pass. Crozier was coming in the other direction and they collided. Crozier wound up with a broken arm and came to practice the next day in a cast." Even then, in his sixties, Joe was as tough as many guys still playing the game.

Things were going well, not only for me personally, but for the team too. Heading into the home stretch of the regular season, we were winning at the same clip we had the previous year. Then, in March, after a couple dozen games with the first line, my season came to a crashing end. Literally. We were playing a road game in St. Catharines, and we had a set play where our defenseman would shoot the puck in hard off the end boards at the exact moment that our forwards tore in on goal after the puck. The boards in St. Catharines, were stiff and the puck would rebound in front of the net where the forwards would be waiting for it. The timing had to be perfect for the play to work, but we had pulled it off with success on a bunch of prior occasions. When we tried to execute the same play on this night, Craig Muni of the Saints aggressively charged at our defenseman, causing him to hesitate before throwing the puck in. This delay threw off everyone's timing, forcing all of us forwards to stop awkwardly at the blue line to avoid being offside. Then Muni hit our d-man with a solid hip check. Our guy went ass over tea kettle and crashed onto my leg. That was it. My MCL was torn.

It was a tremendously disappointing way to end my season. Our team's greater disappointment came in the Calder Cup Finals. The Maine Mariners, who we were favored to beat for the second straight year, got their revenge and beat us, four games to one.

I watched the playoffs in a cast. After my surgery, I was told not to expect to return to the team until December at the earliest. I couldn't imagine waiting that long. They took my cast off in May. I lived with our team's broadcaster, Tom George, during that summer and I rehabbed like a madman. At one point, I couldn't straighten my leg out all the way because of the buildup of scar tissue so I placed some phone books under my knee and used my body weight to force my leg straight. It hurt like hell and I could hear the tissue tearing, but my leg straightened out. When training camp began at the end of the summer, I was there.

TWENTY-FOUR

I NEVER LIKED HURTING PEOPLE. Of course, during my playing days, that probably wouldn't have been the most helpful admission a player who earned his living by fighting could have made, but I just never got off on injuring an opponent. In fact, Charles Kuralt of CBS News once described me as, "slow to anger, like a gentle Ferdinand the Bull." While I didn't like to hurt people, I did want to eat. And I did want to keep playing hockey. I also knew that if I wanted another shot in the bigs, I had to dominate the rough stuff while I was in Rochester. So, whether I liked it or not, I was consciously aware that my greatest opportunity would come from wrecking people. It was pretty obvious that the coaches and scouts weren't going to notice me unless they saw someone bleeding. Fortunately, the AHL was loaded with quality opponents for Ferdinand to gore.

Dave Brown was one of the all-time tough guys to come through the AHL. He exploded on the scene with the Maine Mariners and quickly built up an impressive resumé of knock-outs. I always enjoyed meeting the new champion in waiting and many of these guys were sure to introduce themselves to me. In my first encounter with Dave, I was disappointed that he never offered a word of greeting before looking to mix it up with me. In warm-ups, instead of saying hello, he stretched out alongside the penalty box, staring daggers at me the whole time. Then, when the game started, we bumped each other a bit and he dropped his gloves, giving me his meanest glare. All this without offering me so much as a "How do you do?" I smiled at him and skated away, leaving him to get the only penalty.

After serving his time in the bin, Dave skated up to me again. "I understand if you don't want to fight me. I have been on a tear here, and you probably don't want to get hurt." This was still not the most formal introduction, but it was enough to now accept his invitation.

The referee, Don Koharski, saw what was coming and warned us, "Don't even think about it, boys. I'll toss both of you." I responded, "Oh, but we have to go, Ko, this young man just called me out. I have to defend my honor, don't I?" Don just smiled and gave us some room. Then I hammered the big guy. His eye was swollen shut before we even reached the penalty box. As my old teammate Chris Langevin said, "Valmore put Dave Brown to sleep that night."

Proving that good manners can be learned, I was flattered to hear that Dave later told interviewers that I was the toughest fighter he ever faced. Not too shabby considering that he fought them all — and beat most of them too.

Another thing I found to be in bad taste were cheap shots. All was fair when we were face-to-face. The sneak attacks and stick work might have bought you an advantage at the moment, but it came at the price of your honor. It also came with an added cost the next time we met up.

One night, we were playing the Fredericton Express up

in their building. Their big defenseman, Terry Johnson, was knocking the shit out of our talented center man, Jean-François Sauvé. J.F. was giving away at least 10 inches and 50 pounds to Johnson. Despite his enormous size advantage, Johnson still saw the need to hit J.F. from behind, knocking him hard on his ass. I was sitting on the bench in my regular spot next to our trainer, Jim Pizzutelli. As he often did when the other team was taking liberties, Coach Keenan stomped over to where we were sitting. "Someone's gotta put an end to this bullshit with Johnson, Pizza." Pizza looked at me and I nodded.

Not surprisingly, Pizza can best fill in the story from here. "Val went out on the next shift and said something to Johnson. They dropped their sticks and gloves, and Val blasted him once in the eye. Johnson was dazed. He skated over to the wrong bench. When he got to our bench, I saw that Val had badly cut Johnson. That one punch had cut him both above and below his eyebrow, and the cut was so deep that the eyebrow was hanging off his face like a bloody caterpillar."

Of course, you can't win them all. I fought another kid in Maine named Paul Mercier. He bull-rushed me at the end of the game and his gloves were off before I even saw him. He surprised me and busted my nose. The home-team locker rooms in the AHL had the better trainer's facilities, so Pizza brought me into the Maine room to patch me up. I was lying on the table in the Mariners room with my eyes shut while Pizza sewed me up. While I was lying there, the Mariners came in after the final buzzer and someone yelled out, "Good, the nigger got cut." My eyes flew open wide and I tried to jump off the table with Pizza's needle hanging out of my face. "Let it go, Val." Pizza told me to stay put and finished the stitch job.

The team doctor came in and twisted my nose back into place, without anesthesia. The crack of my nose echoed through the room and I never once broke my stare at the Mariners players peeking through the open doorway. None of them would return my eye contact.

I'd assumed that the kid who cut me had made the slur. "Pizza, I'm going kill that fucking guy." It turns out that it wasn't Mercier who had said it, but I was still livid. After calming me down, Pizza called out to the Maine trainer, who he didn't like anyway, "That's some low-class bullshit your guy pulled." They "fuck you'd" each other and went their own ways.

I wasn't used to coming out on the short side of a fight. All these years later, my teammate Mal Davis can still recall the effect it had on me that night. "Val had never lost a fight, ever. This was the only time that Val didn't get the better of an opponent in a fight. He didn't lose this one in Maine badly, but the guy did get the best of him. It was a shocking moment, for Val and for the rest of the team. I always sat on the bus with Val and he was just so down after that game. He was so disappointed. The whole team was just as somber as he was. I told Val, 'Just dust yourself off and get back at it.' We were still on the bus ride home and Val was already getting himself ready for the next time we would play Maine."

The next time our teams met was a couple weeks later. Everyone knew what was coming. Keenan hated the Maine coach. Pizza hated the Maine trainer. And I wanted to avenge my earlier loss and offer payback for the disrespectful slur from the anonymous coward in the Maine locker room.

For their part, the Mariners were super high on this kid Mercier and his performance in our previous bout. They clearly saw it as a changing of the guard. Early on in the rematch, Mercier was put on the ice and Keenan sent me out. I stepped up to him and said, "OK, now let's try this face-to-face." We dropped the gloves and I landed my first punch square between his eyes. That blow was fueled by every ounce of frustration and fury that I had bottled up since our last meeting. There was the loudest "WHAP" when I connected with his skull. You could hear it in the cheap seats. Mercier's arms dropped to his sides and his eyes clouded over immediately, like the eyes of a corpse. He was there, but not there. I could have destroyed him, but he was completely defenseless. It would have been like beating on a child. I skated away.

The next time I saw Mercier, he came over to me in warm-ups and thanked me for pulling up in our fight. "I knew you were pissed off at me for that night so thank you for not laying into me when you had the chance."

I had been frustrated that this kid had beaten me, but I had redeemed myself and there was no need to hurt him any further once his defenses were down. Geordie Robertson recently reminded me of another night when I eased up on a different Maine opponent. "We had a game up in Maine. I was in the penalty box and Val was on the ice. Val squared off with this enforcer named [Marc Andre] Marchand on the Mariners. Val grabbed this guy and hit him with a quick one in the head. I heard a loud snap when Val's fist hit his head. Val cocked back his fist again but then he stopped and just skated to the penalty box without throwing another punch. In the box, I asked Val what happened. Val just said, 'I hurt him.'"

Geordie continues, "After the game, there was a knock on the door to the Americans' locker room. It was this guy Marchand. He still had most of his gear on and he wanted to talk to Val.

Val went out into the hallway and we thought they were going to resume their fight. Instead, Marchand shook Val's hand and thanked him for pulling up in the fight. He said that when he was hit with that first punch, he saw three Vals standing in front of him and he was scared he was about to get killed. I thought they both handled themselves with a lot of class."

I would very rarely take an extra shot on someone once I had taken away his defenses. Whenever I had a guy down and out, as with Mercier or Marchand, my mind flashed to a game I saw when I was playing juniors in Quebec. Back then, our Remparts team shared the Quebec Coliseum with the Nordiques of the WHA. The Nords players were our mentors and our friends.

Late in my first season in Quebec, we went to the Colisée to see the Nords in a playoff against the Calgary Cowboys. Marc Tardif of the Nords was the best player in the league at that time, maybe the best in the world. Nobody on the Cowboys could skate with him, so their enforcer, Rick Jodzio, decided to take him out. Jodzio chased down Tardif and hit him hard, high, and from behind. The way Marc fell, you could tell that he was unconscious before he hit the ice. But Jodzio wasn't satisfied with disabling the best player in the game. He jumped on Marc and started punching him in the face until Marc's teammates, and ultimately the police, rushed in to break up Jodzio's assault. By the time the cops restored order, my Remparts teammates and I had run down to the boards and were seconds away from jumping into the fray in our street clothes. I'm all for fighting in the game, but where is the honor in beating on a defenseless player?

As much as fighting itself, intimidation certainly played a big role during my time in Rochester. Mike Keenan believed in getting a psychological advantage. He wanted to put fear in our opponents, even before the game started. Mike had the perfect accomplice in Pizzutelli.

Over the years, Pizza made up boxing robes for me, Chris Langevin, Lou Crawford, Mark Wichrowski, and Don Keller. My robe was white with blue trim and had my name spelled out in big letters on the back. Lou had "LOU DAWG" on the back and Wichrowski had "WITCHY" on the back.

Pizza had us wear the robes on the ice while the opposing team was warming up. Pizza would introduce each of us in his best Howard Cosell voice, "In this corner, weighing in at 210 pounds, from Long Island, New York, the undisputed heavyweight champion of the world, Valmore 'Chocolate Thunder' James!"

We must have looked like lunatics out there, wearing our boxing robes and staring down the other team. We were sending a not-so-subtle message about what they could expect in the game that night. Pizza knew that getting in the other guy's head was half the battle, and he loved it.

Pete Rogers reminded me of some more of Mike and Pizza's head games. "In Rochester War Memorial Arena, the visiting team would have to walk past the Americans' locker room. Mike Keenan left the door open and had Val punching the heavy bag in the open doorway as the other team walked by. Val was so big and strong that the heavy bag was jumping and bouncing all over the place. The other team was scared to death seeing Val pound the shit of this bag. They had to be wondering if that's what he had in store for them during the game."

Another night, in Sherbrooke, I went out to the bench area while Sherbrooke was doing their pregame skate. Jim Wiemer remembers what happened next. "Val went out there with no shirt on. He was so big and strong, so cut. He started yelling and carrying on, calling out the other team. They all skated away from him. They wouldn't come near his side of the ice. Those guys had to be thinking, 'Man, this guy is nuts, I don't want to deal with him tonight.' The coach started Val at center that night and he ran right over the other team. He really shook them up. He was so intimidating that we won that game in the pregame skate."

As our broadcaster Tom George says, "Keenan specialized in psychological warfare. When he put Val on the ice, it completely threw off the timing of the other team. You could see their players looking over their shoulders, wondering, 'Oh no, where is he?'"

Of course, intimidation only goes so far unless you can back it up. At one point while I was on Rochester, my old coach and friend, John Brophy, took over as coach of the Nova Scotia Voyageurs. Brophy was no stranger to intimidation tactics. Nova Scotia had some tough guys on their team. Their main heavyweight was a juicer, but I dropped him quickly when we met. The next game we played against them, Jeff Brubaker had taken over their top enforcer role, so I guess he thought it was his turn to take on the league champion.

We lined up across from each other and I watched the linesman, waiting for him to drop the puck. Just before the puck was dropped, Brubaker slid closer to me and I saw that his gloves were already at his fingertips. I could see his knuckles and I realized this prick was going to try to suckerpunch me. I was game to go with anyone, at any time, but that kind of cheap shit always pissed me off. Big time. When the puck dropped, I surprised Brubaker by being ready for him. After I hit him with a quick right hand, I got a hold of his sweater with my left. I then returned to my right and hammered him senseless. The fight was over quicker than my anger could fade.

In the penalty box, I barked at Brubaker, "A big fuckin' guy like you and you gotta try to suckerpunch me?" From the other side of the box, he told me to fuck off and, for good measure, he threw in a too-common racial slur. I had been pissed off by his attempt to cheap-shot me; now I was enraged.

The penalty boxes in the War Memorial Arena were side by side and were separated by a sheet of plywood that was bolted into the steel frame. The attendant in our side of the box that night was my buddy Rollie, an off-duty Rochester cop moon-lighting in plainclothes as the penalty box gatekeeper. Seeing my rage, Rollie tweaked me, "You gonna let that punk hide behind a little piece of plywood, Val?" In my fury, I figured that Rollie had a good point.

I grabbed the plywood and yanked it off with one tug, the bolts tearing free and flying across the box. The penalty box attendants jumped out onto the ice, in fear for their lives. I tossed the plywood aside and it was just me and Brubaker in what was now one double-wide penalty box. Brubaker's eyes grew wide as I charged at him. After a few blows, I had him on the floor but I was still seeing red. He got a hold of my jersey at the wrists to keep me from cocking my arms back, so I grabbed him by his ears and slammed his head up and down, over and over, bouncing it off the concrete floor. Coach Keenan and the linesmen climbed in the box and jumped on my back and, somewhere in the back of my mind, I could hear Mike yelling, "Stop it, Val! That's enough! Stop it!" I could hear in his voice that he thought I might very well kill this guy. I let up on Brubaker and allowed the linesmen to lead me off the ice. Our fans were going berserk. So was our trainer, Pizza.

I was given a major misconduct penalty and thrown out of the game. (There was no penalty box left to put me in anyway.) The league suspended me for a couple of games and fined me a few thousand dollars, but the fine was paid by the team as was stipulated in my contract. The fans in Rochester always treated their team well and we rarely had to pay for meals or beers while out on the town but, after the penalty box skirmish, I had to turn down rounds of drinks because there were so many coming.

There is no doubt in my mind that my old friend and mentor, John Brophy, had sent Brubaker after me. Hell, if I was him, I would have done the same thing. I just took issue with the attempt to cheap shot me. That dirty shit always made my blood boil. Then the racial slur pushed me over the edge.

I got a similar earful of racist bile the first time I encountered a particularly rambunctious rookie goaltender in Hershey. Every time I skated past his crease, this future All-Star jabbed at me with the butt end of his stick. We hadn't met before so I asked Junior if he might have a problem that I could help him work out. The rookie said that he didn't have a problem, but he did have a question, "I was wondering what a nigger was doing out here on a hockey rink. Did you lose your basketball?" The insult wasn't particularly original. Then again, neither was my response: I tried to strangle the scrawny prick. He was spared the beating of a lifetime only because I managed to get my skate caught in his net. Fighting on one foot, the goalie and his two defensemen probably tagged me more than I did them. But I certainly got the hotshot's attention, and his future trash talk was noticeably free of any racist taunts.

There were still a few guys who tried to make up for their inability to hurt me with their fists by trying to do so with their filthy words. I can tell you that none of them did that more than once. Pizza can sum up the reason for that, "There was a lot of racial taunting of Val. Mostly by fans and some by opposing players. But the shit from opposing players stopped quick when Val started punching guys' eyebrows off."

TWENTY-FIVE

"VAL JAMES PROBABLY CAN PLAY for the Amerks as long as he desires." Or so wrote *Times-Union* hockey columnist Bob Matthews after we won the Calder Cup in 1983. "Every team needs an enforcer and Prince Val is one of the best."

Bob's suggestion, that I might wear an Americans sweater for many years to come, certainly sounded like a good plan to me. I loved playing and living in Rochester. But things can change awfully fast in hockey. I didn't know it at the time but, just over one year after our Cup celebration, I would be heading into my last season wearing the red, white, and blue.

My hopes were high as I arrived at that training camp in the fall of 1984. I had shaven three months from the doctor's prediction for my return from knee surgery and my intense rehab schedule had me in excellent shape for the new season. Our team was coming off back-to-back appearances in the Calder Cup Finals. Unfortunately, we were no longer being led by Coach Joe Crozier, who returned to his well-deserved retirement, but we were excited about our new coach, Jim Schoenfeld. Jim was a tough and respected former Sabres captain. He had us fired up about the coming year.

A strong start to our season matched our high expectations. We lost only six of our first 25 games and Jim had our team in first place. However, Jim missed being on the ice and, shortly before Christmas, he turned in his whistle and clipboard and returned to play for the Sabres. His replacement was John Van Boxmeer. I can't imagine that it is easy to replace a successful and popular coach mid-season, but our season flattened out completely once the change took place.

John went on to coach the Americans for nine years, but he had been retired from playing for maybe five minutes when he replaced Schoenfeld. Some brand new coaches go too far in trying to show everyone that there is a new sheriff in town. This is especially true when the coach himself had very recently been playing for the same organization as many of the players who were now subordinate to him. Most of the guys on our team knew John, either as a teammate or an opponent. I felt that he went overboard in trying to break that connection, in trying to show us that he was the boss.

John demanded that we play hard at all times. I had no problem with that philosophy. I was used to playing for demanding coaches like Brophy and Keenan. I had rehabbed myself back onto the ice much faster than the doctors thought possible. Hard work was the path to everything I had achieved in my life. Still, somehow I wasn't working hard enough for John's liking. He wanted me to kill everyone, all the time, yet he was a guy who tiptoed in the corners when he played. John sat me in the press box as often as he played me. The 55 games I got in that season were the least action I saw in any of my four years with the Americans, including the previous year when I tore up my knee.

It's hard to describe that season as anything but a colossal disappointment. After such a promising start, our team barely played .500 hockey the rest of the way. Coming off two straight appearances in the finals, we managed only one post-season win against Baltimore before they knocked us out of the playoffs in the first round. There was indeed a new sheriff in town. I realized, with a heavy heart, that it was time for me to move on from Rochester.

I signed with the Toronto Maple Leafs organization and was assigned to their AHL affiliate, the St. Catharines Saints. The coach in St. Catharines was former Leafs defenseman Claire Alexander. He was starting his second season at the helm of the Saints, but that first year had been a complete disaster, with St. Catharines finishing in last place. Claire was a decent man, well respected, but he was very laid back. In fact, I had that same first impression of the Toronto organization as a whole. "Play hard? Haven't you seen the hockey history books? We're the Leafs. We're fuckin' royalty. Why should we have to play hard?"

Not surprisingly, we started the season right where the team had finished the previous year, in last place. A number of weeks into the season, the front office in Toronto decided it was time for a change in St. Catharines. They turned the team over to the Leafs' assistant coach, John Brophy. Needless to say, Brophy did not believe in resting on the organization's ancient accomplishments. He gave us every bit of the jolt that you would expect to get from John Brophy.

Unlike the mid-season coaching change we had in Rochester the previous season, Brophy was a shot in the arm for our team. We won six of his first seven games behind the bench. We spent the rest of the year clawing our way out of that early-season hole, and we clinched a playoff spot in the closing days of the campaign. I played every game that season, including the play-offs, spending a total of 215 minutes in the penalty box along the way. At the same time, my former team in Rochester missed the playoffs for the first time since before I had played there.

In the first round of the playoffs, we played the Binghamton Whalers. Binghamton finished six points ahead of us in the regular season, but we were on a roll from our late-season scrap to reach the playoffs. We beat Binghamton, four games to two.

Next up was the first place Hershey Bears. They were 10 wins and 18 points better than us during the season. In fact, Hershey was a huge favorite to win it all. They had made light work of New Haven in the first round and were expected to do the same to us. However, our series would quickly turn into a seven game war. We went down three games to one but fought back to even things up and get us back to Hershey for a winner-takes-all finale.

As far as toughness, the Bears were, well, loaded for bear. They had guys like Steve Martinson, Andre Dore, Don Nachbaur, and Carl Mokosak. But, for my money, Mike Stothers was the toughest of their lot. During that seven game series, I fought Mike no less than 13 times. He was a big, fearless fighter under the best of circumstances. To make a tough job even harder, I broke my right hand on Mike's helmet in the first of those 13 fights. I had to keep my fist buried in a hidden bucket of ice during every minute of the series.

I certainly had my hands full with Mike. Each of those fights was tougher than the last. We battled every step of the way. No one wanted to give an inch. Recently, Mike captured perfectly a sequence of three separate fights that he and I had during a single bench-clearing brawl at the end of Game 2:

"There was a big fracas between the teams. Val and I fought

and we pounded each other good. After a while, that fight broke up, but then things started heating up again, so Val and I got back at it. We started hammering each other again. We wound up fighting against the boards, next to the penalty box, and we were both beat. Paul Stewart was the ref that night and I see Stewie skate over to us. I'm thinking to myself, 'Good, get in here Stewie, I'm exhausted.' We were just in a war, actually two wars, and my arms were really heavy, just exhausted. But, instead of breaking it up, Stewie grabs the two of us and says, 'C'mon boys, out to center ice and let's finish it.' So we went at it a third time at center ice."

After seven games of trying to kill him, I finished that series with nothing but the utmost respect and admiration for Mike. He stepped up, time after time after time. When you battle a man in that way, you can learn a lot about him. I learned that Mike was an honorable man who always represented himself and his team with guts and dignity.

Game 7 itself was a tight contest, with fewer fights. Unfortunately, we came up on the short end of the score. That's one loss that still bothers me to this day. I don't know if the officials were tired of taking Brophy's shit but every call seemed to go against us that night. The offside calls were bad enough, but we also had two goals disallowed. I scored the last goal in our 4–2 loss.

As bitter as that loss was, I was proud of myself and my team. We were written off for dead before Brophy ever showed up. Still, we refused to surrender and we nearly toppled the league champs before we were done. I also got a charge playing all those road games in Hershey. If you didn't get fired up playing in the old Hershey Arena, then you better check your pulse. Their fans loved hockey and they loved their team, much like the fans in

Rochester. During the infrequent lulls between my battles with Mike, I would hear the Hershey fans chanting, "We want Val! We want Val!" I guess 13 fights wasn't enough!

It was a much different atmosphere in St. Catharines, where our hometown support was pathetic. The playoff games held in Hershey were packed with 4,500 screaming fans. Even after playing weeks of winning hockey, the playoff games in St. Catharines might have drawn 1,000 patrons. We lost a pair of close games at home during that series. It certainly didn't help that there was no home field advantage to be had in our own building.

At the end of the Bears series, the fans in Hershey gave me a nice hand. When it was all finished, I was exhausted and sore as hell, but I suspect that Hershey felt the same way. It took everything they had to beat us and, as a result, they were spent when they played Adirondack in the Finals. Adirondack, who had finished with seven fewer wins and nine fewer points than Hershey, defeated the Bears, four games to two.

The lackluster support the Saints received in St. Catharines resulted in the team being moved to Newmarket the following season. For whatever it was worth, the move meant that my final goal against Hershey would be the last ever scored by a member of the St. Catharines Saints. The move also meant a new home for me for the second time in two years. I was in St. Catharines only for that single year but I will always remember the town fondly because it was there that I met my soulmate and future wife, Ina.

I first spotted Ina at the Grape and Wine Festival that is held each year in St. Catharines. My eye was immediately drawn to her amongst the crowd of thousands. I tried to make it over to where she was but she vanished into the sea of people attending the Fest. Seeing me frantically search through the throngs, a buddy asked me what I was looking for. I told him, "I just lost the woman that I'm supposed to marry."

A few days later, I was skating in a Saints pregame warm-up when I saw her again. Ina was in the stands with her friend, Cindy. Cindy worked with children with mental disabilities. That night, Ina and Cindy were chaperoning a group of kids to the hockey game. During the game, I was working up my courage to approach her as soon as the final buzzer sounded. However, they left before the game ended and, again, I had missed my chance.

As fate would have it, opportunity would knock one more time. I wasn't going to blow it again. After our game, I went to a local tavern to unwind with my Saints teammates. And there she was. Ina and Cindy were seated at one of the tables. Ina was not much of a hockey fan so, when she saw us come in wearing suits, she assumed we were Jehovah's Witnesses. That is, until we ordered our first round of drinks. There wasn't a teetotaler amongst us.

Ina and I hit it off right from the start. She is beautiful, smart, and witty as hell. I was smitten. And I still am. After the team left St. Catharines, Ina agreed to accompany me to Newmarket, and I have been blessed to share with her all the journeys ever since.

TWENTY-SIX

FEW PEOPLE IN HOCKEY have treated me better than John Brophy. And to be sure, few people have treated me worse either. When Brophy showed up in St. Catharines, he was to become my coach again for the first time since I was a teenager and Brophy was helping Sam Gregory run our Met League team. As he had been during my earliest years of playing hockey, Brophy was also an enormous influence on me during my time with the Toronto Maple Leafs organization.

I knew Brophy since I was a little kid following my dad around the Long Island Arena. In fact, I can't remember a time in my life when I didn't know him. In my earliest memories, Brophy was menacing the old Eastern Hockey League as a member of the Long Island Ducks. As mentioned earlier, he was something to see on the ice in those days, a cyclone of fists, stick blades, and white hair. He wasn't at all a big guy, probably a couple inches under 6-foot. He was also older than most of the other players on the Ducks, and he looked older still with that full head of premature gray. He played almost all of his 20-something years in the EHL, most of it at a time when the NHL had only six teams. Hockey in the EHL was every bit a blood sport, and the "Gray

Ghost" was the most infamous of its many legendary villains. In his time, Brophy spent better than 4,000 minutes in the penalty box. And it wasn't because he was wrongly accused! Of course, he was also one of my earliest role models.

Brophy and my dad were very close, although you wouldn't know it if you happened to see their act in person. They were always ripping into each other. They barely spoke without breaking balls and cursing out one another. People would be shocked at what looked like hostility on the verge of punches being thrown, but they were actually close friends and they spent a lot of time together. As recalled by one of my oldest buddies, Greg Martinelli, "Brophy and Henry James had a different kind of relationship. They were always arguing and yelling at each other. If you didn't know them, you would think they hated each other, but they were very tight. They were very fond of each other and they had great respect for each other." That's all true, but they sure did make for an odd couple.

Brophy recently laughed when sharing one of his memories of my old man. "Henry James had a Doberman that was always at the Long Island Arena. Henry said it was his pet. That dog wasn't anybody's pet. That was the meanest dog that ever lived. It guarded the arena at night. One time, the Ducks came home from a road trip at 2 a.m. and some of our players went inside the arena to catch some sleep. The first guys in the building could hear the dog running up. It was growling with its nails scratching on the concrete, so they ran and locked themselves in a phone booth. The dog wouldn't let them out and, since they had the keys with them inside the booth, no one else could get in the arena. They had to call Henry from the payphone so he could rescue them from his crazy dog."

Brophy was a complicated man. He was both the kindest and the harshest of men that I've ever known. He was not someone who gave his players a lot of slack. And my dad's history with Brophy never bought me any extra leeway. In some ways, he made things harder on me than on his other players . . . not that any of them had it easy.

My first reunion with Brophy happened the first time Rochester faced his Nova Scotia Voyageurs. I was having a good night hammering some of Brophy's tougher players. The whole first period, he was growling across the ice at his team. "That black bastard is killing you fucks! Knock him on his goddamn ass already." During a break in play, I skated over to the Voyageurs bench. His players thought I was about to kick their coach's ass. Instead, I offered him a big smile. "Hi Brof, it's good to see you." Brophy stuck out his hand, "Hey, Val, you're looking good. Keep playing hard out there." His players were blown away to find out that we knew each other.

In St. Catharines, when the laid-back Claire Alexander was replaced by the . . . less than laid-back John Brophy, he ran us ragged from the beginning. We did drills where we had to climb over the glass from one penalty box to another, a practice Brophy knew something about from his own playing days. He also loved to have us run "crushers," skating from line to line, back and forth, and then finishing each set with 25 pushups. Your body would tremble from head to toe as you struggled to do that last push-up. The whole time, Brophy was yelling his special form of encouragement, "Move your fat asses, you lazy fucks!" Some of the players hated him for it. But I knew Brophy — and I knew what was coming. Within 30 days of him becoming our coach in St. Catharines, I was in the best shape of my life. But getting there was no party.

When I started my year with St. Catharines, I was solid from a summer of working out. But once Brophy was hired, he only saw that, at 218 pounds, I was eight pounds heavier than I was the previous season. He told me to lose the extra weight but, even after intense training, I was still at 213. Brophy then told me I had three weeks to get down to 210. He worked me harder than anyone else. After his typically grueling practice, I would ride 20 kilometers on the stationary bike and then put in another 90 minutes in the gym. At the end of the three weeks, my body fat was down to seven percent. Only Kevin McGuire, with a ridiculous number of three percent, had a lower rate on the team. However, when I got on the scale, the numbers "2 - 1 - 3" were looking back at me, and at Coach Brophy. It was back to the torture chamber for me.

When the team practice was over, and my teammates were dragging their exhausted asses to the showers, my day was just beginning. Brophy started me out with some more crushers, followed by push-ups. Then he had me skate all-out sprints from one side board to the other. Next, he had me skate laps that included more trips over and through the penalty boxes. There's no doubt that his mad plan was working. I was in tip-top shape. My stamina was better than it had ever been. But I still weighed in two pounds too heavy. So Brophy put me in the hot tub and turned the heat all the way up. He cooked my ass for 15 minutes. I lost five pounds. Of course, it all came back as soon as I rehydrated myself. But Brophy's hot tub regimen gave me an idea. My buddy, St. Catharines firefighter Dan O'Brien, ran the Gold's Gym in town. Danny would let me in the place early in the morning before I went to practice. I'd spend some time sweating in the sauna before heading to the rink. When I got to practice, Brophy would be waiting for me at the scale. No problem: 210 pounds, just like he wanted.

More than anything in life, Brophy wanted to win. He wanted us to win our shifts, win our fights, and, of course, win our games. Losing made him nuts. Or more nuts than usual.

One night, we had fallen behind in a game in Sherbrooke and Brophy was not pleased with our effort. He tore into us as we sat quietly in the locker room. He was spitting, "You fucks aren't fuckin' losing because they are better than us, you fucks are fuckin' losing because you're not even fuckin' trying." To emphasize his *fuckin'* point, he picked up the huge chalkboard that was used for drawing up plays, lifted it high over his head, and then slammed it down on his own skull, shattering the board into a million pieces. And that was just his warm-up act.

Covered in chalk dust and chips of slate, Brophy yanked off his sports coat and tore it to shreds. With loose change and the rest of the crap from his pockets flying all over the room, he ripped the arms and the collar off his coat and then he tore the body into rags, all the while cursing up a storm. "If that fuckin' team is better than us, I'll suck cock on fuckin' Main Street at High Noon."

Some nights, playing for John Brophy could be the greatest show on Earth.

There's no doubt that Brophy raised the level of my game. There was no such thing as an off night when he was in charge. Although he never said it at the time, he must have been content with my efforts, because he played me in every single Saints game that he coached. I tried to show him every night that he made the right call. Often, that meant tangling with the other team's designated hitters. I was more than fine with that.

Following our strong finish to the 1985–86 season, the Saints moved to Newmarket and Brophy moved to Toronto. After going through countless yards of sutures during a quarter century of playing in the minors, followed by another 15 years of coaching at the lower levels, Brophy had finally made it to the NHL. As happy as I was for him, I was sorry to see him go. He had put me through hell that year in St. Catharines, but our team had developed a winning attitude when Brophy was our coach. With him now gone, we lost much more than we won.

Personally, I was having another decent year with the Saints. I enjoyed the confidence of our new coach, Paul Gardner, who played me every night. Despite all the losses, I just tried to keep on playing my game. Of course, this typically meant more of the rough stuff.

Storied tough-guy John Kordic provided the challenge on one particular night when we played in Sherbrooke. Kordic was able to sneak a quick one in on me before I was set. In trying to get my feet straight, I slipped and went down to a knee. Paul Stewart and the other official started to come in, figuring that I was about to get killed. After all, how many players have survived being down on the ice with John Kordic standing over them, raining down bombs? But I was able to get my feet underneath me and, in a fierce bout, I punched my way back to at least a draw. Stewie later described the fight in the press, "That one was awesome with a capital AWE."

In the penalty box, I called over to Kordic, "Johnny, you're better than that cheap shit. When we get out of here, let's do this again face-to-face." He agreed, but when we got back on the ice, Kordic was called to his bench by his coach and he skated away. I didn't get the rematch I wanted.

During that same trip to Sherbrooke, I went out for a drink with a few of my teammates. We wound up at a local club called The Triple X, not exactly a family-friendly establishment. While we were there, Kordic and a few of his teammates also showed up. Our two sets of players waved to each other as we sat at opposite ends of the bar. Kordic and his mates had the home field advantage so the gals in the place were paying them more attention than the other patrons. This special attention upset a large group of drunks in the club, who started mouthing off at Kordic and his friends. Seeing our hockey rivals were outnumbered, my teammates and I walked over to Kordic and made it obvious to everyone in the place that we all knew each other. I told Kordic, "We're here if you need us, Johnny." The drunks were suddenly less interested in trouble when the sides were evened up. We might try to kill each other on the ice, but we were going to have each other's backs when we saw these "outsiders" looking to jump the Sherbrooke boys. The drunks wisely thought better of the idea and slunk out of the club.

A couple of months into the year, I would be reunited again with John Brophy, if only for a week or so. Brophy called me up to add some punch to his Toronto Maple Leafs. As with many of my experiences with Brophy, the call-up was both the best and the worst of times.

Of course, hockey is the national religion of Canada. And, at the risk of upsetting some of my friends in the City of Saints, Toronto is the Mecca of that national religion, and Maple Leaf Gardens provided its basilica. My first game for the Leafs came on November 24, 1986, against the Boston Bruins at the Gardens. As the Maple Leafs announced at the game, I was the first black player to ever skate for that historic club. I only got on the ice for a couple of shifts that night. We blew a two-goal lead and we lost the game on a goal scored by the Bruins at the very end of regulation. As you might imagine, that last-second loss put our coach in poor spirits.

Of course, as always, Brophy's practices in Toronto were

hell on Earth. As was the case in St. Catharines, his most severe demands were again aimed squarely at me. When he lined us up at practice for one of his hands-on demonstrations, I would try to hide in the back of the pack, out of his sight. It never worked. "Where's Val? Get the fuck over here." I believed, then and now, that Brophy knew I could take the hardest he had to dish out, and he wanted to use me as an example for the rest of the team. Again, that's not to say anyone got off easy. Still, rarely did I play a game where I was more beat up and more spent than I was after one of Brophy's practices.

In one of these Leafs practices, Brophy pulled together the defensemen to demonstrate the importance of winning battles in the crease in front of our goalie. Brophy chopped at me with his stick and kicked my skates out. Every time I popped back up, he hacked me and knocked me back to the ice. Over and over again. Chris Kotsopoulos and Jerry Dupont got much of the same treatment. In case we didn't get the message, he shouted at us, "You either win that area in there or you don't stay with the hockey club. It's as simple as that." He knew that nothing scared a hockey player more than the idea of being cut. And Brophy hung that threat over the heads of his players every single day.

My second game with the Leafs was played in Detroit. The shiny new Joe Louis Arena was the home of the Red Wings. The Joe itself was located in a much less shiny part of Detroit. The neighborhood would not be considered hockey country. While we were in town, Wendel Clark and I set out to find a bite to eat. We only had to walk about one block before Clark became an endangered species. In other words, he was the only white person in sight. He laughed when I told him, "No need to worry, Wendel, we're with my people now."

The Detroit game itself is best remembered for a collision involving the Leafs' legendary defenseman Borje Salming that took place in front of our net. Salming got kicked by a skate and his face was split in two from his forehead to his chin. By the time he reached our bench, his flesh had opened up like a canyon. His jersey was soaked in blood. It took almost 300 stitches to close up the wound.

Putting aside the gore of the Salming injury, the game did not live up to the expectation of an all-out war, at least from my perspective. The Red Wings had called up their rookie heavyweight, Bob Probert, but Bob was more interested in hanging onto me than trading punches. As Brophy says, "Probert stayed away. It was obvious he didn't want anything to do with Val." Harold Snepsts also spent that whole game trying to avoid me. Willi Plett was another guy who was content to wrestle. I just couldn't get a good chance to show what I could do. Of all the fights I couldn't get that night, Brophy was most pissed off with one that never developed between me and Basil McRae.

Brophy didn't like Basil, not even a little bit. I didn't know it at the time but the previous game between the Leafs and the Wings had included a nasty exchange of words between Brophy and Basil. Basil and I came together during the game but we were separated after some light pushing and shoving. I knew Basil through his brother Chris, who was my friend and teammate on the Saints. I liked Basil and there is no doubt that I could have made short work of him. When I came back to the bench, Brophy was furious. "You should have torn his fuckin' head off!"

Brophy had called me up to Toronto because the Leafs had been getting roughed up by tougher players on the other teams. But it was difficult to get many fights during my time there.

When I was in the AHL, I was someone who always gave the new guy a shot, but it seemed that a lot of guys in the NHL were not willing to give me the same chance. They would rather not fight unless they were pretty damn sure they were going to win. To put it mildly, Brophy felt I should have pushed the issue harder. If I couldn't get a guy to drop his gloves, then he was to be a guy who kept his hands warm while he got his ass kicked. Many fighters were willing to dish out that kind of one-sided beating, but it was never my thing. Looking back, I have no doubt that my reluctance to beat on an unwilling opponent hurt my opportunity to play in the bigs, particularly for Brophy in Toronto.

Shortly after I passed on breaking Basil's neck, we were getting dressed in the locker room when Brophy charged in. He lit into me in front of the whole team. "It's a long fuckin' road to the NHL, but it's a short fuckin' trip back down to the minors." With that, my Leafs career was over.

I don't have any doubt that skating away from Basil cost me a longer look in Toronto. These days, Brophy tells me that it wasn't a factor; he says my return to the AHL was just a numbers thing. Brophy now says that I did everything that he ever asked of me.

Deep down, I think we both know that wasn't the case.

During the 1986–87 season, I became the first black player of any nationality to play for the storied Toronto Maple Leafs organization. That sweater just screams "Original Six."

PHOTO: GRAIG ABEL

Located in Commack, New York, the Long Island Arena was my home away from home. My dad ran all of the building operations, and I grew up working at his side. It was here that I was introduced to hockey. The arena was also home to the notorious Long Island Ducks of the old Eastern Hockey League. Those players became my hockey mentors.

Despite working 20-hour days, my dad, Henry, found time to coach our Hauppauge High School team. He excelled at football while growing up in the South, but he fell in love with hockey at the Long Island Arena. PHOTO: CHRIS BRINSTER

The Suffolk Ducks entry in the New York "Met League," founded by Emile Francis and run by Lou Vairo and John Muckler. It was hockey with a New York attitude. We even played some of our games at Madison Square Garden.

PHOTO: GREG MARTINELLI

As a teenager, I left everything on Long Island to play in Midland, Ontario. I was the only black person in town, and I was the first black that many of them had ever met. That didn't stop the people of Midland from welcoming me into their hearts and homes. The road trips were often a much different story.

PHOTO: JUDY LARMAND SUAVE

Worst haircut competition:
Here I am with Chris Brinster
after our initiation to the
Quebec Remparts. After
Midland, I played two years
in Quebec City. That first
year, we won the league
championship and competed
for the Memorial Cup.

PHOTO: CHRIS BRINSTER

Road trip: A quick pit stop
during a Remparts bus trip.
Notice the baby-faced Kevin
Lowe leaning over in the
middle of the group.

PHOTO: CHRIS BRINSTER

When I played for the
Erie Blades, we won
three straight league
championships. It was a
mutual love affair between
the Blades players and
our home fans.

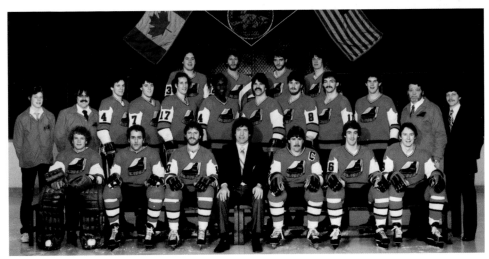

In Erie, our closest opponents were the cross-state Johnstown Red Wings. They were not good neighbors. It was not unusual for the police to have to escort us out of town.

Ray Kurpis and I got together like this many times. Despite these occasional disagreements, I found Ray to be a worthy and honorable opponent.

This was my first full year in Rochester. The following season, with coach Mike Keenan at the helm, we won the team's first Calder Cup in 15 years. I was lucky to play four full seasons in that terrific city.

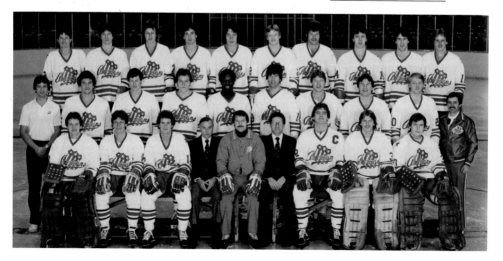

During the 1981–82 season, I achieved my dream of reaching the NHL as a member of the Buffalo Sabres. No American-born black player had ever before reached the show. Not bad for a kid who worked on a farm and got his first skates at 13 years old.

What a long, strange trip it's been: Here I am sitting on the Sabres bench. My role was to keep our opponents honest. Coach Scotty Bowman says, "Val filled that role to a T." Who am I to argue with the greatest coach in hockey history?

My first year with the St. Catharines Saints saw me reunite with my old coach John Brophy. Once Brophy took over behind the bench, we went from last place to nearly upsetting Hershey in the Calder Cup semifinals.

PHOTOS: GRAIG ABEL

The end is in sight. Here I am, in 1987–88, playing a handful of games for the Flint Spirits before being acquired by the Baltimore Clippers. After only eight games in Baltimore, I was blindsided into the boards and tore up my shoulder. After 15 years of junior and pro hockey, it was time to hang up my skates.

PHOTO: DAVID MADELONI

TWENTY-SEVEN

WHEN THE END OF my hockey career arrived, it was delivered courtesy of a rookie who hit me from behind and drove me headfirst into the boards. It was a reckless move on his part, but I knew that he hadn't set out to intentionally injure me. We were both chasing the puck and sometimes these things happen. From the look on his face, he was in shock at the sight of my limp arm, hanging as if detached from its mooring in my shoulder. I wasn't angry at the kid — I just needed him to stop apologizing and get out of my way so I could go see the doctors.

It took some time to get the proper diagnosis, but once it was all sorted out, I knew I was done. And then, just like that, it was over. The Baltimore Skipjacks sweater that the team trainer peeled off my battered body would be the last I ever wore in a professional game. The boarding incident brought a sudden, physical close to my career. However, in my mind, I had already been inching in that direction.

The year prior to sustaining that injury had been my last with the Toronto organization. After Brophy sent me back down to Newmarket, I finished the season with the Saints. Other than the call-up to the Leafs, I didn't miss a single game played by the Saints that whole year. And, the year prior to that, I played in all 93 of the team's games during the regular season and the play-offs combined. The organization had certainly gotten its money's worth out of my contract, which had just expired. I didn't expect that signing a new contract was going to be a problem; I assumed that the team appreciated my hard work and dedication. And, in fact, they did offer me a new contract but, before signing it, I asked if I could speak with Gerry McNamara, our general manager.

I didn't know McNamara very well, but he had been the guy who signed me to the organization when I left Rochester. I also knew his son, Bob, a goalie I played with on the Americans. I told McNamara that I was very grateful for the opportunity the team had given me, but I also asked him whether he could envision me having a role on the team in addition to the rough stuff. There was no doubt that fighting buttered my bread, and it always would, but I had worked long and hard on improving every aspect of my game. Most recently, while playing for the Saints, my teammate Walt Poddubny had spent many hours with me after our team practices, tutoring me on my puck shooting skills. I felt that my game had come a long way over the years. I shared with McNamara my longstanding hope that my fighting ability might lead to opportunities to also test my other hockey skills.

McNamara stared right through me as I spoke. When he finally responded, I wished that he had stayed mute. "If you even try to touch that fuckin' puck, I will bury you so deep in the minors no one will ever be able to find you again."

I walked out of McNamara's office with the unsigned contract still in my hand. His words bounced around in my head. It was clear that loyalty was a one-way street with him. I kept right on walking.

McNamara was the first boss I had, at any level, who told me that I brought no value to the team beyond my ability to punch out other players. Whether it was Nick Polano in Erie, Mike Keenan and Joe Crozier in Rochester, even John Brophy in St. Catharines, each of them had complimented me for my improving play and each had given me additional responsibilities over time. Now, I was being told that, in McNamara's eyes, I was only of use when my gloves were lying on the ice. It was a defining moment for me. I had used fighting as a means to become a more rounded player. I assumed that McNamara had noticed. I was wrong. I left behind a good chunk of my passion for the game in his office that day.

It would be easy for an enforcer to buy the line that McNamara was selling. You become very self-conscious about your hockey skills, and it wouldn't take much goading for you to believe that you were "just a goon," that you had nothing more than a side-show contribution to the game. It is never much of an issue as long as you are winning all of your fights — the fans love you and the organization is content. But there is intense pressure to perform every night, in every fight. Hockey is a team sport but, like it or not, it is the enforcer's successes — and failures — that most often fill the highlight reels.

I am not surprised that many enforcers have serious issues with depression. Sadly, some of them are never able to overcome it. For my part, I would never concede McNamara's suggestion that my calling was limited to hurting other players quicker and worse than they could hurt me. Of course, that was the objective during the scraps themselves, but I was always fortunate to have coaches and teammates who appreciated all of my contributions. I had shown, time and again, that I was willing and able to stand up for my teammates. I also felt that I showed I could play some too. At one point, while I was with Rochester, the *Hockey News* commented that I had developed into a legitimate top-six defenseman. Rochester was one of the elite teams in the AHL at that time. And the NHL only had 21 teams back then, not 30 teams like today. So being recognized as an effective player on one of the top AHL teams was a great compliment that recognized how much my skating and hockey skills had developed.

While I didn't need McNamara's validation, his reaction was a reminder of how I was seen in the eyes of some others who, unfortunately, had opinions that mattered. If more than a decade of hard work and success couldn't change their minds, it seemed unlikely I would be able to do so now that I was quickly approaching my 30th birthday.

I had not expected to leave the Maple Leafs organization so I did not have a backup plan when the time came. I accepted an invitation from Rick Dudley to play for the Flint Spirits team he was coaching in the International Hockey League. I only played eight games in Michigan, scoring a couple of goals and winning a couple of fights. Then I was offered the opportunity to return to the AHL, this time with the Baltimore Skipjacks.

I wasn't sure what to expect when I arrived in Baltimore. When I played for Erie in the EHL, the fans of the Baltimore Clippers had dished out nearly as much racist filth as I faced in any of the other cities that we visited back in those days. As was reported in a *Washington Post* story at the time, "Val James says he gets the most abuse in Salem, but scores of Baltimore Clipper fans demonstrated Wednesday night they are in the same bigotry league. Scattered jeers of 'Buckwheat' and 'Nigger, Go Home' could be heard around the Baltimore Civic Center when James, who scored a goal and assisted on another, took his first turn on the ice in the Blades 7-4 victory."

Despite my apprehension about playing for a town that had shown me so much hate, I needed a job. As it turned out, I was treated well by the fans during my short stay in Baltimore, but my enthusiasm for the game was further sapped by the fact that I even had to consider whether the racist taunts would pick up right where they had left off. For almost 15 years, I had to approach each town, and each game, with at least some consideration of what reaction would be prompted by the color of my skin. I would be lying if I said that, over time, it didn't take a toll. It did.

I was only in my ninth game with Baltimore when my face got buried in the boards. The initial concussion tests were negative so I continued to practice with the injury. Unlike the million previous bumps and bruises, this one got worse as each day passed. It got to the point where I couldn't lift my arm, not exactly a positive development for a professional hockey player, let alone a hockey enforcer. The team called in Dr. Thomas Whitten, a specialist in sports medicine. Dr. Whitten injected a dye into my shoulder, which finally identified the problem. When I'd collided with the boards, there had been a severe tearing of the muscle in my shoulder. However, because the tear went north and south along the muscle, it was not visible on the x-rays. Dr. Whitten did a fine job sewing things back together, but I was sidelined for the rest of the year. My mind and body were starting to agree on the nagging question of whether I should retire.

Before I left Long Island to attend my first pro camp with the Detroit Red Wings, I had a long talk with Sam Gregory. Sam was a former Long Island Ducks player and was one of my hockey coaches and mentors as I was growing up. Sam was sharing some advice on how I might best take advantage of the opportunities that lay before me. He also said something that seemed out of place at the time, "When the time comes to call it quits, you'll know it. Don't ignore the signs. If you stay too long, you're gonna get yourself hurt. If you stay too long, they're just gonna make you go anyway. When you leave, you want to do it on your own terms. Not when someone else tells you it's time to go."

I was just setting out on my hockey career and Sam was telling me to be ready to recognize the end when it arrived. It seemed an odd time to bring it up, but as I sat in Baltimore with my arm immobilized for eight weeks, Sam's words came back to me. He was right, I could see it. It was time.

A couple of years after I retired, Ina and I went to Erie for a reunion of our EHL championship teams. As fate would have it, John Brophy was in town with his Hampton Roads Admirals. We were waiting for the hotel elevator to open, and when it did, there was Brophy. He grabbed me in a big bear hug. "Hey, Val, you look great. Let's get you signed and we'll have you in the game by tonight." Brophy told me not to worry about being rusty. "Look, you just have to skate long enough to grab someone and kick his ass. Then you can rest for five minutes at a time." I told him I wasn't up to it.

Truth be told, I was tempted to get back on the ice but I knew that my Erie hosts would have responded poorly to one of their guests of honor accepting an invitation to attend a celebration, only to turn around and beat the shit out of their beloved home team. Brophy let it go but, before he got back on the elevator, he passed his phone number to me and said that the door was open in Virginia if I ever wanted to get back in the game. And then, just like that, the elevator closed and he was gone. More than 20 years would pass before I next spoke to John Brophy.

TWENTY-EIGHT

JUST LIKE EVERY OTHER young black child born to southern sharecroppers, I dreamed of playing professional ice hockey . . .

OK, so maybe I was the only one of us with that particular dream, but at least it made sense to me. I was not put off by the fact that, when I was growing up, American-born players made up less than five percent of the National Hockey League. Nor did I see any reason to be discouraged that no American-born black player had ever skated in the world's premiere hockey league. My mom and dad were similarly unfazed by these inconvenient factual tidbits.

To my parents, the object of my dream wasn't important, no matter how far-fetched it might seem to others. Whatever my dream was, they were going to support it completely, simply because it was *my* dream.

When I started skating, I set out to be a hockey player, not a black hockey player. However, the two concepts quickly became intertwined. And not by choice. From early on, there were some people who were determined to prove to me that being black and being a hockey player were mutually exclusive. And I was just as determined to prove them wrong, by any means necessary.

One of the many activities that my family made it possible for me to attend was the series of hockey camps in which professional players and coaches instructed us on the finer points of the sport. Each summer while I was growing up, I was eager to go to these camps but I also knew that none of them were cheap. Fortunately, many of the camps were held locally at the Long Island Arena, where my dad ran the physical operations of the facility. With the camps held on home ice, my dad could cut deals with the people running the programs. On special occasions, I was also able to attend sleep-away camps. These camps cost big bucks, yet my parents somehow found a way to send me to a fair number of them.

In my early teens, my folks arranged for me to attend Dennis Hull's hockey camp in Illinois. Because two of my aunts, Maxine and Ellen, had settled in Chicago, I was able to stay with them, making the camp more affordable. The camp had a strict rule prohibiting fighting, with automatic expulsion as the penalty. During our scrimmages, one older camper repeatedly goaded me, calling me a nigger every time I came near him. I tried to ignore the taunts, reminding myself, over and over, just how difficult it had been for my folks to pull together the money to send me there. My anger finally overrode my concern of disappointing my family.

The kid ran his mouth one more time and I filled it with my fist. I jumped on top of him and tried to punch every ounce of racism out of him before the instructors, all hockey pros themselves, pulled me off. This wasn't the first time I heard that word on the ice. It was, however, the first time that I answered with my fists. No other response would ever seem adequate. Dennis must have agreed. He investigated the cause for the fight and gave me a pass. The older camper was the only one sent home.

When I returned to my Aunt Ellen's home that evening, she was less impressed that the camp had given me a pass. When I told her of the fight, her concern was not with the other camper or his cutting insults. She said the ignorance of others was something we could not control. Instead, she was disappointed in me, to put it mildly. She really pinned my ears back that day.

In a reflection of her southern upbringing in the middle of the twentieth century, my aunt expected that, as a young black man, I should control my emotions. She was disappointed in me for letting my anger and pride dictate my actions.

To my Aunt Ellen and many in her generation, the harder and smarter response to racial taunting was to walk away. Although she didn't say so, I think she was really afraid of what could happen to me if I responded to racists. I was more concerned with what would happen if I didn't. I would never say that my wonderful aunt was wrong, but in the incident with my fellow camper, I had tried to walk away. That didn't stop him. He stopped only when I stopped him, with extreme force.

Going forward, when an opposing player took to calling me a nigger, walking away was never going to be my response. I know that my aunt only wanted to see me raised the right way, but if my opponent's own upbringing didn't teach him that it was unacceptable to treat me that way, then I was willing to deliver that lesson to him myself.

Being black never prevented me from playing professional hockey, but my race was certainly a factor in me being pigeonholed solely as a fighter. Back in the 1970s, when I was coming up, the Canadian powers that ruled hockey looked upon most big American players as instruments of brute force. Look at guys like Chris Nilan, Nick Fotiu, Ed Hospodar, Paul Holmgren, Paul

Stewart, and myself. The thought was that, while the Yankees might be able to offer some mindless muscle, why would Canada need to look beyond its own borders for any real hockey talent?

If big American players were seen, first and foremost, as hired hatchet men, how do you think I was viewed? I was big, American . . . and black. There was not a lot of thought given to developing my overall game. Sure, I took advantage of my physical skills and my fighting ability to land a spot at the table, but then once I was there, I put in every effort to develop into a more rounded player. At each level, I gained the confidence of my coaches, but when either the coach or I moved on, I was back to where I started. "Oh yeah, that's Val James, the big, black, American player who can kick some serious ass."

While I was not prevented from playing hockey because of my race, it did make the path harder, angrier, and lonelier. A black hockey player was a duck alone on an island. I could go a full season without seeing another black hockey player. More than that, even seeing a single black fan in the stands was a rarity.

When a Salem newspaper did a story on me, they tried to find a black person to interview at the game. They had to settle for talking to one of the security guards. In Erie, the management of the Blades encouraged me to reach out to the small black community in town. The team gave me complimentary tickets to give away, but I had trouble convincing black folks that I was a hockey player. "C'mon, we all know that there are no Negroes in ice hockey." It was hard to argue with that sentiment.

As a black player, even my own locker room could sometimes become a lonely place. Throughout my career, I was blessed to have had teammates who always welcomed and supported me. I was never made to feel anything but a complete part of every team on which I played. However, things would get very uncomfortable whenever I was subjected to racial abuse. Fully intending to be supportive, my teammates would often tell me to ignore the taunts as merely the words of the ignorant. But, unlike the rest of the team, I was the only one subjected to these words. The words themselves were hurtful only to me. Even amongst my brothers in the locker room, I was made to feel alone.

For a time, I did have a teammate who could understand that, to a certain extent, I would always be an outsider. My last year in Rochester, I had the honor of playing with Ted Nolan. Ted was a smart, tough player who would later go on to excel as a head coach at every level at which he was given the opportunity. Like me, Ted did not fit the "mold" of what a professional hockey player was supposed to look like.

Playing with Ted was one of the very few times in my career that I had a non-white teammate. Ted was Native-American, having been born and raised on the Garden River First Nation Reserve, just outside of Sault Ste. Marie, Ontario.

Like me, Ted was often the target of racial insults and taunting from the opposing fans. Where I might hear, "Hey monkey, go have a banana," Ted would hear, "Hey Injun, want some firewater?" or some similarly vile snipe. It happened far too often. There wasn't much we could do about it but at least Ted was another guy who understood that these slurs were not "just words." They meant so much more than that. These slurs were spit at us as a mocking reminder that our ancestors were once enslaved and considered to be less than human.

Ted and I were the only ones on the team who could really appreciate just how cutting the taunts were. I was sorry that Ted had to go through the same harassment as I did. However, it made the abuse somewhat easier to take when there was someone else on the team who could truly relate to your experience.

When we played on the road, my presence on the ice brought out the worst in the opposing crowds. Some nights, they would get so worked up that I thought the whole place was going to keel over with one massive stroke. Visiting enforcers are already natural villains. The fans love their own enforcers but hate those of the other team. My black skin only seemed to ratchet up the vitriol. The sight of a black hockey player, who was also adept at kicking the ass of their hometown heroes, was just too much to take.

I make no apologies for being a hockey player who didn't hesitate to use his fists. Hockey is a contact sport; since the beginning, fighting has always been a big part of it. Hockey without fighting is something less than what the sport has been for over 100 years.

Let the fans be the judge of what role fighting should have in hockey. The next time you see a fight during a game, take a look around the stands. You won't find a single ass planted in the seats. They are all on their feet. The fans get charged up. The players get charged up. A good fight can change the momentum of a game as quickly as a goal.

While fighting can provide a needed spark, it can also have a calming effect. It may sound backwards but I am convinced that fighting actually reduces violence in hockey. If you have no fear of getting your lights punched out, you're more likely to carry your stick high or to take a shot at the head of a more skilled player. Fighting helps keep the game honest.

One of the problems in hockey today is the lack of respect that players have for one another. Of course, there were always players who had no respect for their opponents but there was a significant price to pay for it back in my day. If you took a dirty shot on one of my teammates, you knew that I was going to beat you into next week. Nowadays, you have all these visor babies, yapping and acting tough. They hide behind their big bucket helmets and the rest of the armor that now serves as equipment. They also hide behind the rules that prevent the policemen from being a deterrent. When everybody is a tough guy, then nobody is.

In my playing days, most professional hockey players did not make enough money to get them through the year, let alone to set them up for their post-hockey life. I worked a variety of off-season jobs, everything from being a bouncer at local clubs to construction work. However, when my hockey career ended, my resumé showed little more than a knack for knocking out players who made the mistake of messing with my teammates. For all intents and purposes, my academic education ended when I left home at 16 to play hockey in the junior leagues of Ontario and Quebec. Fifteen years later, when I hung up my skates, there was no pension waiting for me.

I now live my life much as my dad did. Like him, I earn my way by the strength of my back and the sweat of my brow. I always wanted to impress my old man. I was made strong through the hard work that I put in alongside him, first on the farms and later at the Long Island Arena.

After many years as a migrant farm worker and sharecropper, Henry James became the heavily relied upon jack-of-all-trades at the arena. In some ways, I have come full circle with the work my dad once put in. While his hard work assured the smooth operation of a major sports and entertainment facility, my hard work goes a long way towards the smooth operation of a large family resort. Also like my dad, I work right alongside the men I supervise, and I would never ask them to take on any task that I would not do myself. I put in hard, honest labor for a day's pay. It was good enough for the man who was my hero when I was growing up, so it's good enough for me.

To many people, the color of my skin was the thing that most identified me as a hockey player. At first, I resisted being seen as a black hockey player. Looking back now, I am very proud of what I accomplished in hockey, both personally and as a black man.

When I was playing, I did not want to be seen as being different than any other hockey player. But, as I was constantly reminded, I *was* different. That difference was shoved in my face at every turn, by my opponents and, more often, by their fans. Many of these fans were outraged that a black man, no less an American black man, had the audacity to encroach on their snow-white sport.

I was told repeatedly that the reason that I could not achieve my hockey dreams was because I was African-American, although much cruder terms were used to describe my race. The record up to that point certainly seemed to support that claim. Even today, very few American-born blacks have succeeded in this sport. None had done so when I started out. The louder the insistence that it could not be done, the more determined I was to succeed. Of course, when the moment arrived and I became the first American-born black player to skate in the National Hockey League, the doubters were silenced. But they were not alone in their silence. There was no official acknowledgment of the moment by the league, either then or since. And that's just fine. My old man didn't need to hear any special announcement to know that I had achieved my dream. He expected it all along.

Thirty years ago, when I was interviewed by Charles Kuralt

of CBS Television, he asked me what I thought was needed in order for race relations to truly improve. I told Mr. Kuralt that, more than talk and good intentions, it would take concrete action for things to change. What type of concrete action? In that 1981 interview, on videotape, I offered the prediction, "Maybe in a few years, things will change. Maybe you will have a senator who is black and he will have a chance to become president."

What was I thinking?

A black president?

An African-American in the NHL?

I'm not sure which was the bigger long shot back then. But a young man can dream, can't he?

EPILOGUE

"AS OTHERS RECALL IT"

JP Dellacamera, Long Island Cougars director of public relations, Erie Blades broadcaster

I knew Henry James when I was the PR director of the Long Island Cougars and Henry was the rink manager of Long Island Arena. Henry was an honest, hard-working man. Val's core values come from Henry. Val would hang around the rink as a kid. His dad fell in love with hockey and his passion was passed on to Val.

Tom George, Rochester Americans broadcaster and radio personality

Val was very conscious of his race, very aware of being a black kid in a white sport.

Jocko Cayer, EHL trainer

Val overcame all the obstacles that came with being a black American trying to make his way as an ice hockey player in the 1970s in rinks up and down the East Coast. The strength and mental fortitude that it took for him to succeed in that world was incredible. He gave 110 percent effort all the time and nothing less would have been enough. No one worked harder. He earned everything he got.

Greg Martinelli, Suffolk Ducks player, Long Island Arena employee

I don't think Val was exposed to much racism on Long Island when he was young. He was just one of the guys. None of us kids at the arena had two nickels to rub together. We were all in the same situation, just working and playing hockey.

Lou Vairo, Metropolitan Junior Hockey Association co-founder

Val was young when he came to the Met League, but he was a big, strong kid. Because of his size, people expected him to fight so he did, but he was not a bully. Val would fight anyone, but he never took advantage of a player once he was down.

Val and his dad, Henry, were very close. I admired Henry. He worked at the Long Island Arena and drove the Zamboni for the Ducks games. He was a hard-working man who did everything for his kids. He lived to make a good life for his children.

I remember Val's little brother, Hank. He was a fun little kid. And he could eat. When the Nathan's in Coney Island saw the bus come in with the hockey team from Commack, Long Island, they knew business was going to be good that day. Hank could eat six hot dogs and six hamburgers in one sitting — actually, in one *standing*, because there were no seats outside of Nathan's.

Greg Martinelli

In the Met League, in a game at Abe Stark Arena in Coney Island, one of the Brooklyn Stars players called Val a "nigger." This other guy had a reputation as a tough guy and there was talk that he had a boxing background. Val ate him up. He stayed away from Val after that beating. After a couple fights, word got around and not many people wanted to fight Val. By the time he was 15 years old, he had a reputation as someone not to be messed with.

John Brophy, Suffolk Ducks coach, St. Catharines Saints coach, Toronto Maple Leafs coach

Val was one of the toughest guys in hockey. He had a tough job. And he did his job, that's for sure. Val knocked a lot of guys out. He was a folk hero. Fighters on other teams would want to talk to him. They would seek him out in warm-ups. Nobody wanted to mess with him. He would sit on the end of the bench and hang his arm over the boards. His hand damn near reached the ice. All the players on the other team would hope he would stay there. Val being there changed the minds of a lot of guys who had bad ideas. If he was on the ice or on the bench, everyone on the other team would settle down.

Judy Sauvé Larmand, daughter of Midland Flyers manager Ron Sauvé

When Val came to Midland, he was the only black person in the whole town. There was about 10,000 people living there but there were no black people at all. We knew absolutely nothing about black people. We didn't know what to expect. The Midland Flyers were a huge deal in town. The players were local celebrities. This meant that Val, like the other players, became familiar with many of the local people. He was the first black person many of them ever met. They got to know him and like him. He was just one of our hockey boys, our Flyers. Val was a positive presence in our lives. Not just for our family but also for the town.

Tom Shields, Midland Flyers radio broadcaster

By Val's second or third game, we didn't discuss his race anymore. He was a crowd favorite. He was personable — he always had a big smile for you. And he wouldn't hesitate to straighten out troublemakers on the other teams. Val and the other Americans just became part of our home team.

Tom Hasenzhal, Suffolk Ducks player, Midland Flyers player

I don't recall any racial incidents when we were on Long Island, but that changed when we went to Canada. In Ontario, there was a strong animosity towards the American players but there was a special distaste for Valmore because he was black. Even though I was there, I don't know how Val was able to take all the extra abuse he got because he was black. What he endured and overcame made me very proud of him. Any lesser of a man could not have done what he did.

Chris Brinster, Suffolk Ducks player, Quebec Remparts player

In Quebec City, our opponents didn't want to upset Val. They would say, "Let the big black guy sleep. Don't wake him up." Everybody ducked him, so he didn't have a crazy amount of penalty minutes. These French-Canadian players who didn't speak a word of English would timidly skate up to Val before the game, "Hello, Mr. James, it's a lovely evening tonight." They wanted to get in his good graces before the puck was dropped.

Kevin Lowe, Quebec Remparts player

Val was a complete gentleman, very likeable. People would be surprised how mild mannered he was. He had a good wit and always had a huge smile. As tough as he was, he was never mean hearted or mean spirited.

Val's role as enforcer developed over time. I don't think it was something he set out to do. But he was highly respected in that role. In fact, he was feared by opposing players around the league.

Val could be made angry. He would get angry if someone hit one of us dirty or did something low or disrespectful to us or to the game. The times that I saw him get mad, it was truly scary.

Chris Brinster

The strange thing is that Val was pushed into being a fighter. He didn't start out looking to make his way in hockey that way. He wanted to play hockey. He fought when he had to or when he was pushed into it. But no one was tougher. He was a real tough guy who only fought other tough guys. Some of these other guys were phony tough guys, they jumped everyone. If Val had fought in juniors as much as he did later on in the pros, he would have been drafted much higher.

Nick Polano, Erie Blades coach

Val was recommended to me by Ben Kasper, who was the owner of the Erie Blades. Ben had been the owner of the Long

Island Arena and he said that Val was a tough kid and a great person. I never scouted Val but I gave him a tryout at camp based on Kasper's word. Kasper didn't let me down. Val was a great team player. His teammates loved him.

JP Dellacamera

Val was as tough as advertised. I don't think he ever lost a fight. His fights didn't last long. He was so strong and so methodical in his fights that nobody wanted to test him.

Guys were afraid to go into the corner with him. If they did, they weren't coming out with the puck. He was so big and strong that he could hurt you accidentally. He definitely had the fear factor going for him.

Nick Polano

We had a very good team in Erie. We won three league championships. That's because we had good players who were also good people. That was Val. He was a major part of that. He was a special person, a complete gentlemen off the ice. He always agreed to speaking engagements and hospital visits, whatever was asked of him.

Robin Roberts Jr., Erie Blades broadcaster and assistant to general manager

Val was very important to the championships we won in Erie. To win a championship, you needed a guy who could take care of the rough stuff. There were some mean, nasty players in road cities like Syracuse and Johnstown, but these guys didn't want any trouble with Val. Val solved all our road problems. But he wasn't one of those sadistic fighters who liked to hurt people. He was a gentleman. He never got any misconduct penalties.

Paul Mancini, Erie Blades player

Val has the longest arms I've ever seen. He'd fight guys and they couldn't get near him. He would get a hold of them with that left arm and once he locked that arm out, they were done. Then he would just pound away, hammering them with his right fist.

The funny thing is that Val was really a mild-mannered guy. He could take a lot of crap. But if he saw someone taking liberties with one of his teammates, then look out. If someone was trying to hurt our players, then he took great offense and that guy was getting hurt.

Gene Ubriaco, coach, Baltimore Clippers (EHL), Baltimore Skipjacks (AHL)

One of my guys in Baltimore [EHL], Bennett Wolf, was a real tough guy, just a special player. Bennett and Val fought each other all the time. Probably too much. One game against Rochester, Bennett had a shoulder injury but he insisted on playing. I told Bennett that I didn't want him to fight that night but his history with Val made that unlikely. So I pulled the rest of our team aside and told them if Bennett went with Val, then they were to jump in. Before the game started, I wrote a letter to the league. In the letter, I laid out our defense for why our guys had to jump in during the fight. The letter was all ready to go out right after the game, but that turned out to be the one time that Bennett and Val didn't fight each other. So the letter went in the trash.

Nick Polano

Val was one of the toughest guys of all time. We had some smaller skill-players, and nobody messed with them because of Val. Val was our equalizer. His fights were over quickly. Nobody could hit him. He just destroyed guys. He has the longest arms I've ever seen. He could throw them with both hands. As far as the tough stuff went, Val was scary good.

Jocko Cayer

Val came to play against us in Salem during my first year with the team. The fans went crazy. As a Canadian, I just hadn't seen that much racism firsthand. A fan told me that Erie had some nerve coming into Salem with a "nigger" on their team. I asked him why he would talk like that about a hockey player he never met, and the guy said, "Down here, the niggers are below us and they always will be." When Erie came to town, the fans made a run to the local supermarket to buy watermelons so they could throw them on the ice like the fans throw octopus on the ice in Detroit.

Brent Gogol, EHL and AHL player

Val James was a warrior. You never had an easy game when you were playing against him. He was a hard player to fight. He was powerful, very strong, and well built — tough as hell.

When we played against each other, I didn't like Val one iota. You could even say that we hated each other. It was a rare night that we didn't go at it at least once when our teams played each other.

Val's race was never an issue for me. He was just another hockey player, and when we fought, he was just another hockey player that I wanted to beat. But sometimes you would hear some of the racial catcalls yelled at Val from the stands, so I knew he was going through it. One of the reasons I was popular in Baltimore was because I would fight this jet-black player on Erie. There's no doubt about that.

Jim Doyle, Met League player, AHL referee

I first saw Val when we both played in the Met League. I played for the Bergen Maulers and Val played for the Suffolk Ducks. I didn't know much about Val back then except that he was very big and very tough and I had no interest in mixing it up with him.

I started seeing Val again in 1980–81 when I was a referee in the AHL and Val came up to play for Rochester.

Val was a warrior. He had huge hands, really enormous. Any time he dropped the gloves, he just punished people. But when the other guy went down, Val was done. He didn't hit guys when they were defenseless. He didn't sucker punch guys. There was no dirty stick-work from him. He was an honest player. He respected the code of conduct that the enforcers lived by back then.

As an official, I appreciated a guy like Val. You knew what his job was and you knew when he was on the ice. But you also knew that he wasn't going to ambush someone behind the play. He handled his work face-to-face and when it was over, he took his five minutes in the box without any complaining.

Val was the kind of guy you would root for because he came up the hard way and earned his chance honestly.

Mike Keenan, Rochester Americans coach

It was fun to coach Val. He wanted to contribute every night. He was always ready, always willing. He could tell if we needed a spark or a charge.

Val's most valuable skills were his team skills. He protected his teammates. Val's presence was a serious deterrent, he kept the other teams honest. He mastered his role more than any player in the AHL. That was a big part of his role on the team and he did it as well as anyone in the league. That is a tough role to fill every night, but Val embraced it. And his teammates embraced him for it. He was a very positive influence on our team.

Barry Meisel, hockey correspondent, Binghamton *Sun-Bulletin* and *The Hockey News*

In the early 1980s, I covered the Binghamton Whalers for the Binghamton *Sun-Bulletin* and was an AHL Southern Division correspondent for *The Hockey News*. Binghamton had a fierce rivalry with Rochester, and the fights were the story of the games many times. Sometimes it was because of the fights Val started. Sometimes it was because of the fights Val finished. The first time I stepped into the Amerks' locker room to interview Val, I figured I might as well try to form a connection before he told me to buzz off for asking why his punching the lights out of some Whaler turned the game around. He was a New Yorker from Long Island; I was a New Yorker from Brooklyn. I expected an ornery enforcer to give me one-word answers because I was from Binghamton and the "enemy." Instead, I found myself talking to an engaging guy whose personality off the ice looked nothing like his intimidating personality on the ice.

Val wasn't just respectful and professional, he was engaging. He was a joy to talk to. He clearly got it. We only saw each other a few times a season, but he became one of my go-to guys on the Amerks. He was interesting, honest, and quotable. It was all a reporter could ask for. It's why decades later, when we found each other again, we were able to smile, tell stories, and remember the New York connection. It's why I am proud to call him a friend.

Ted Nolan, Rochester Americans player

Val had a feared reputation long before I ever met him. As your opponent, Val was an intimidating force. Just to see him was intimidating. When you prepared to play against Rochester, you were well aware that Val was on their roster. When he was in the lineup, everyone knew they would have to play an honest game.

Once I got to know Val, it was funny to see how everyone was so scared of him, because I knew he had a gentle soul. He wouldn't hurt anyone if it could be avoided.

Jim Pizzutelli, Rochester Americans trainer

If you fought Val, something was getting broken. He hit like a sledgehammer. He was a good guy, but if you got him mad, someone was getting hurt. Someone would be missing games. We would say that these guys were out with the "Val James flu."

Val was not a goon. He would never sucker punch anybody. He wasn't one of these guys who would grab anybody and start punching them. He wouldn't look to instigate a fight. But he was, by far, the toughest guy in the AHL in the years he played there.

Paul Stewart, pro player and NHL official

Val James is the toughest guy I've ever fought. He was hard to hit and hard to hurt. I always respected Val. He was big and strong and was always game, always willing to go.

Val respected the game and the code amongst the tough guys. You had to respect your opponents. You needed them in order to be able to compete and they needed you the same way. Our opponents gave us a chance to prove our reputations and to earn our pay. You could not be a tough guy unless you fought other tough guys. So you needed each other.

There was a certain chivalry amongst tough guys. You didn't take advantage of another guy if you got him down. It was like the dogfight pilots in World War I. If one guy ran out of bullets, the other guy would fly alongside and give him a wave before flying away. Val was a guy who always played this role with dignity and respect.

Mike Stothers, AHL player

Val was the toughest man in the AHL in that era. He was so strong, such a big man. His build and the strength he had made him a very hard guy to fight. He was a ridiculously hard puncher and he was the ultimate competitor.

You could never truly beat Val James in a fight. You would think to yourself, "If I can survive this, that itself would be a victory." Maybe you could hope for a draw. I would consider a draw or a close fight with Val to be a victory.

Scotty Bowman, Buffalo Sabres coach and general manager

We had a lot of skilled players in our organization, in Rochester and in Buffalo, but we needed to get tougher. Val filled that role to a "T." He was a very rugged player. He was so tough and so strong that he was able to put out a lot of fires for us. We used to say that Val kept the flies off his teammates.

JC Ihrig, Rochester Americans stick boy

To me and the players on the team, Val James wasn't black, he wasn't white, he was just one of the guys. He was just part of the team, and he was a big part of it. If you knew him off the ice, you would have no idea what a fierce player he was. He was always happy, always smiling. In fact, whenever I hear Val's name, I can't help but smile.

Tom George

During one playoff series, the Hershey Bears were in Rochester to play the Americans. Val had a number of friends on the Bears, and Val and I invited them to go out for drinks the night before a game. We even provided them with door-to-door transportation. We loaded up my Lincoln with a bunch of the Hershey players and we all went to a local pub. Val and I fed the Bears guys pitcher after pitcher of Genesee Cream Ale, a locally brewed adult beverage that, when consumed in excess, is known to cause severe indigestion and diarrhea, known in these parts as "the Genny Screamers." The next day, all of our guests from the previous night cursed us as they skated by the bench. The Americans crushed the Bears that night. You might say that Genny squeezed the shit out of them before the Americans beat the shit out of them.

Mike Stothers

Val had the league belt and if a new guy wanted to prove himself, he would have to fight Val. Val was always willing to give them the opportunity but, still, a lot of guys didn't want to tangle with him. He didn't have ridiculously high penalty minutes. That's because a lot of guys preferred to let him sleep. He was a lot like Clark Gillies in that you didn't want to make Val mad, you didn't want to wake him up and have him coming after you.

When he played in the AHL, Val had a reputation as the toughest guy in the league. One thing I admired about Val was that he got that reputation honestly. He never pulled any cheap shots, there was no dirty stick-work, no eye gouging, no jumping guys. That dirty stuff went on back then, but you knew you wouldn't be getting that from Val.

Val's job was to protect his teammates and he did that very well, but he never took advantage of smaller guys and he never hit guys who were down or vulnerable. Val always matched up against other big guys, guys of equal size and ability. When you played against Val's team, you knew what was in store for you. He always went toe-to-toe. He played honest and he played hard. He was known as a great teammate.

Mike Keenan

There were a lot of tough players in the league back then. A lot of heavyweights. Val James was the best of all the heavyweights in the league. No one was tougher.

Mal Davis, Rochester Americans player

Val was really the heart and soul of our team. He was one of the best team-players I ever saw. If we were having a bad practice, he would settle things down. There is a lot of pressure in hockey. Your job depends on your performance. Practices can be as intense as games. You need a guy like Val, a real impact player, who set a positive tone for everyone else.

In the locker room, Val had a tremendous presence.

When he walked into the room, the atmosphere immediately changed. The whole team would get positive and upbeat. He was such a positive, inspiring influence in that room.

Val's teammates loved him. We were thrilled he scored the game-winning goal when we won the Calder Cup. That had to be the most celebrated goal in team history.

Chris Langevin, Rochester Americans player

Val got better as a player every year. He was a late bloomer and he was still developing. He worked hard and consistently improved his play. I think he was best as a defenseman. The other team would avoid his side of the ice. That gave them a lot less room to play in.

Geordie Robertson, Rochester Americans player

Back then, both teams would skate warm-ups between periods on the whole length of the ice. I would skate with Val and if one of our opponents had been taking shots at me, I would point right at the guy and loudly say, "That's him, Val, that's the guy there." The other guy would look at Val staring at him and have a heart attack. I wouldn't have any more problems that night. You always knew that Val was going to straighten things out. Guys on the other team would see me and Val together and figure, "Oh, we better leave Geordie alone."

Mal Davis

A lot of guys didn't want to fight Val. Val had a heavy punch, his punches hurt. Even when he wasn't on the ice, he had a calming effect on the other team. If he was going to miss a game for an injury, we would say suit him up anyway and let the other team see him on the bench. They wouldn't know any better. But, then again, Val wouldn't be able to get any of those free hot dogs they had up there in the press box.

Brent Gogol

In 1984, I was out of pro hockey for three years and working in the oil fields in Calgary when Glen Sather signed me and sent me to the Oilers AHL club in Nova Scotia. I played in a handful of games when Nova Scotia was next scheduled to play Rochester. Some of my teammates were talking about having to play "CE" and I asked them who CE was. They told me that CE was Val James. He had been nicknamed the "Career Ender" because fighting him could mean the end of your career. I told the guys that I had fought Val a bunch in the EHL and I was looking forward to a rematch. Unfortunately, I was scratched right before the game and we never had that one last fight.

Tom George

The Americans were rock stars in Rochester in those days. And none was more popular than Val. It was a love fest between Val and the fans.

One summer, Val lived with me at my house in Rochester. He let a kid try on his Calder Cup championship ring. The kid ran off and Val couldn't chase him because his knee was still wrapped from a recent surgery.

The same day the ring was stolen, a bunch of Rochester police officers pooled their money together and put word on the street that they were willing to pay a reward for the return of the ring, no questions asked. The officers were big fans of

Val and the Americans. Later that night, the officers came to my house and returned the ring to Val.

Ted Nolan

Val was a solid chunk of a man. His hands were so big. You would look at them and think, "Can you imagine getting hit with those?" Not too many guys wanted to tangle with Val James. He was a modern day assassin. Nobody wanted to get him upset. He was so powerful and so strong that he didn't have to fight most of the time. Knowing he was there was enough.

Pat Meehan, EHL, AHL and NHL referee and U.S. Congressman

I knew Val well when I was a referee. He was a great fighter, known in every town. He was also a class guy. The Eastern Hockey League played in Virginia. I was the ref during a game in Richmond between the Richmond Rifles and the Erie Blades. Some fans behind the penalty box had a monkey doll with a noose around its neck. When Val went to the box, they waived it at him. I saw them do it. I told the PA announcer to signal to security that it had to stop. They told me there was nothing they could do. At that point, I told them to contact someone with management. I wasn't going to drop the puck again until those fans were removed. If they wanted to find another referee, they could do so, but I wasn't working until those fans were gone. After a few minutes, they took them away and so the game continued. I could have been disciplined for what I did but I thought that if I saw what they did, and I did nothing about it, I was just as bad as them.

Geordie Robertson

After playing in Rochester, I played in Adirondack and Val went to St. Catharines. We lined up against each other for a faceoff. I said to Val, "No. 7 on Sherbrooke keeps hitting me dirty. If it happens again, you and me are going to have a problem." Val laughed and skated away.

The next time we played Sherbrooke, No. 7 skated over to me, "Why are you sending Val after me? Don't get him pissed off at me." No. 7 didn't bother me anymore.

Joe Crozier, Rochester Americans coach

Val was a very tough guy and a player who always looked out for his teammates. He was a fan favorite in Rochester.

I did a weekly segment on the Wednesday night newscast in Rochester. Each week, we were teaching kids how to play hockey. The show was very popular. One week, I brought in some of our tougher players, including Val, and we did a show on how to win in a hockey fight. I told the kids in the audience that the number one rule in a hockey fight was to get in the first punch. Well, we got some grief over that. But it was true. And it still is. You do have to get in that first punch.

Chris Langevin

The AHL was a very rough league. Every team had at least one or two guys who could handle the rough stuff. You needed those guys so your stars could play. No one wanted to fight Val.

I never saw Val James lose a fight. Val's fist was huge. It was easily a size and a half bigger than mine. His presence, even on the bench, was enough to keep the other team on good behavior. His glare was enough. That glare was something to see.

I'm just blessed that I got to know Valmore by playing with him and not against him.

Ted Nolan

When you think of the Rochester Americans, you think of Val James.

John Brophy

While the other team practiced in warm-ups, Val would stand at the entrance to the ice naked from the waist up, wearing nothing but his skates and hockey pants. He stood there and stared at the other players. He was enormous, all muscle. He looked like Superman. The other team would skate by and think, "Oh brother, am I gonna have to deal with this guy tonight?"

Paul Stewart

I tried to get Val into officiating after his playing career was over. At the time, I was an official in the American Hockey League and Val was still playing for St. Catharines. I said to Val, "Can you imagine the two of us working a game together? No one would give us any trouble. We could put the whistles away."

Brent Peterson, Buffalo Sabres player

Scotty brought Val in because we had problems with the Boston Bruins. Nobody really wanted to fight Val. He was so big and tough. You had to be pretty brave to go with him. Val was on a line with Larry Playfair and Lindy Ruff. It was a line of defensemen playing as forwards. It's pretty impressive when Lindy is the least toughest guy on your line.

On the road, some fans would yell racial insults at Val. He

would try to ignore them. I don't recall any opponents using racial slurs with Val when he was with Buffalo. If they did, they were either very stupid or they had a death wish. He would have cleaned up on someone if they said that garbage to his face.

Mike Stothers

Val was a good, honest enforcer. He played hard between the whistles and when it was over, there was no trash-talk or bashing, just respect.

He was an extremely tough man, but more than that, he was an honest, honorable player.

I have a lot of respect for him. He didn't have an easy time in his career. He did it the hard way. And he made it without taking any shortcuts.

I think about Val a lot. I never heard any more about him after hockey and I often wondered how he was doing. I will never forget the many encounters we had. He made me a better player. He made me a better competitor. He made me a better teammate.

I would love to meet up with Val someday, only next time we keep our gloves on!

Kevin Lowe

Val would have had a better chance today for a longer career in the NHL. He had not been playing hockey very long when he came to Quebec, but with his size and strength, more time would be spent now developing his hockey skills.

The fact that Val was able to succeed in hockey stands as a great testament to him as a person.

It was hard enough for anyone to make it to the NHL, but

it was harder for Val, not only as one the few Americans back then, but as a black player. Then he did it the hard way, working his way up through the different minor leagues. He really hung in there. He persevered. When I saw he made it to the NHL, I was very proud of him.

Lou Vairo

He probably doesn't know this but Valmore James was a huge inspiration to me. What he did with his life, against the odds, inspired players and coaches to move on to other levels of hockey. The battles and struggles he had to overcome were enormous. It was rare for an American to excel in hockey back then, but a black American? It was unheard of. He faced the ultimate test of character and will. And he flourished. I just admire him greatly. He should be very proud of all that he accomplished.

AFTERWORD

WHEN I DECIDED TO write my life story, I didn't know what reaction to expect. Would anyone remember me from my playing days? Would those being introduced to me for the first time find my story valuable? In short, what would the response to this old hockey player crawling out from under his rock (as my wife likes to put it so gently) actually be? Shortly after the publication of *Black Ice*, I was surprised and honored by the tidal wave of positive feedback that quickly put my doubts to rest.

The day after *Black Ice* was released, Pat Borzi of the *New York Times* wrote a feature story about my life. My wife said that the *Times* photographer made me look like a movie star. Who am I to argue with my wife? Pat's article was followed by coverage on National Public Radio, BBC, *Canada AM*, ESPN, Fox News, CNN, and many other major media outlets.

Within days, I was invited by the Rochester Americans to a celebration they were having in my honor. The team had scheduled a Val James Night. A *Val James Night*? As my friends back in New York might say, "Who'da thunk it?" What a thrill it was to return to the town where I had some of my greatest hockey memories and made friendships that have lasted more than 30 years. That magical evening in Rochester kicked off a year of celebration and happiness beyond anything I had dared to hope for. Yet, as often is the case when achieving something worthwhile, the road was not without bumps.

While writing *Black Ice*, I had experienced vivid flashbacks to the days when I earned a living playing the great sport of hockey. Growing up, all I ever wanted was to be a hockey player. Writing about the happy times I shared with family, teammates, and friends brought many smiles to my face. But with the good memories also came the bad.

Like watching a movie, the process of writing about my experiences caused me to relive the many nights I had spent pretending I wasn't bothered by the slurs and insults flung at me because of the color of my skin. When those taunts filled one arena or another, I had been able to hide the fact that they hurt me far worse than any check my opponents could dish out. But the hurt lingered. For many years after I hung up my skates, I couldn't even watch a hockey game on television without flashing back to contorted faces spitting their hatred. I could still hear the echoes of their jeers. So I pushed the memories deeper and deeper inside.

During my playing days, I swore I would never let the ignorance of others drive me from the sport I love. Little did I know how successful they would be in driving me away from hockey for so long after I retired.

I also failed to realize how much these memories could still cut me when I finally pulled them from the place I had buried them for so many years. When I did, I was back in the moment. I relived the same sadness, the same anger, the same loneliness. And putting these stories on paper was also painful to my beloved wife. Ina is my partner and my closest friend, but she was hearing most of these stories for the first time. (Her response tells me that she could have been a heckuva enforcer herself.) I soon realized that not only had I not shared these stories with my wife, or anyone else, but I also hadn't truly faced them myself.

If I was going to tell my story, I was going to have to drop the gloves with an opponent I loathed — and feared — more than any I had ever encountered on the ice. That opponent was the anger, the hatred towards those who had tormented me, that I carried in my gut.

To finally face off against the ghosts of racism that still haunted me, I reached back for a lesson my folks taught me many years ago. My parents, who grew up in the Jim Crow South, raised me and my siblings to appreciate the value of forgiveness. The value to the forgiver, as well as the forgiven. We were taught that without forgiveness, you have nothing. I couldn't control what others said or did. But I could control whether or not I forgave my agitators. I held that power. And I used it so I could let go of the bad feelings that were living inside of me. Forgiving is harder than hating. But forgiveness heals, while hatred corrodes.

One of the reporters who interviewed me about the book asked what lessons I hoped to share in writing *Black Ice*. I responded, "I wanted to write a truthful book and the truth can be painful at times. I had to open up a lot of old wounds. I want to make people think about things they could change in their own lives in order to make themselves better people and make the world a better place. I had to learn to forgive. And it took me a while to get to that place. I'm hoping people come away from this book realizing that a little bit of kindness can go a long way." It is kindness from others that made it possible for me to reach my dreams.

In the end, sharing my story was cathartic. The bad experiences no longer fester inside of me. I am honored by the feedback from readers who have had similar experiences and have found strength in my tale. I reunited with family and friends, who for too long had only been part of my past. I reconnected with my former teams and teammates and recalled the strong support and many acts of friendship they offered me over the years. I made new friends, including the great Willie O'Ree, a boyhood idol and true pioneer. I have been reintroduced to the sport I love, and I have been given the opportunity to share what I've learned with kids, particularly kids who look like I did growing up, for whom hockey is a new sport. Much good has come from sharing my story. Now, more than ever, I look forward to the next chapter.

ACKNOWLEDGMENTS

JUST AS THERE ARE too many people to adequately thank for their support of Val during the years that he pursued his dream of playing professional hockey, there is no way to sufficiently recognize all those who helped turn Val's life story into this book. Perhaps first amongst the many is our editor, Michael Holmes, and all the folks at ECW Press who believed Val's story was worthy of wider telling, and then helped two rookie writers navigate through every step of the publishing process.

Another indispensable friend has been Brian Hyland, the esteemed documentary producer, who knows as good as anyone how to spin a sports yarn and how do it so the most people hear it.

A number of photographers, both pros and friends with cameras, have graciously shared the photos seen in this book, including Mark Mattson, Dave Madeloni, Chris Brinster, Greg Martinelli, Judy Larmand Suave, and Ray Kurpis.

Thank you also to singer and songwriter Johnny Wakelin for use of the lyrics to his hit song, "Black Superman."

Friends whose media expertise helped the process along include John Miller of CBS, Rich Funke and Todd Hayes of WHEC in Rochester, New York, as well as writers Matt Birkbeck, Barry Meisel, Marc Zirogiannis, and Erie historian/author Chuck Pora.

Invaluable research assistance came from the Society of International Hockey Research (www.sihrhockey.org); the Historical Society of Lebanon County, Pennsylvania; and the public libraries of Midland, Ontario, and Salem, Virginia.

More support came from family and friends, including Matthew Elwood, who helped Val type out his notes, and Big Earl Skakel and Anthony Pagano, who helped gather video resources and were reliable soundboards for our developing ideas and drafts.

To all these folks, and many others not mentioned here, we thank you from the bottom of our hearts for making this book possible.

VALMORE JAMES was born in Ocala, Florida, and raised in Long Island, New York. After 15 years of junior and professional hockey, Val hung up his skates and settled in Ontario, Canada, where he and his wife, Ina, recently celebrated their 25th wedding anniversary.

JOHN GALLAGHER was born in New York City, where he worked as a police officer and an assistant district attorney. He later served as a White House Fellow in Washington, D.C. John now lives with his family in Philadelphia, Pennsylvania, where he works as a federal prosecutor.